FORM AND DESIGN IN CLASSIC ARCHITECTURE

COMPOSITION BY JOSEPH BONOMI

FROM AN ORIGINAL DRAWING DATED 1784 IN THE POSSESSION OF THE AUTHOR.

FORM AND DESIGN IN CLASSIC ARCHITECTURE

Arthur Stratton

DOVER PUBLICATIONS, INC.
Mineola, New York

Bibliographical Note

This Dover edition, first published in 2004, is an unabridged republication of *Elements of Form & Design in Classic Architecture, Shown in Exterior & Interior Motives Collated from Fine Buildings of All Time on One Hundred Plates,* originally published by B. T. Batsford, Ltd., London, in 1925.

Library of Congress Cataloging-in-Publication Data

Stratton, Arthur, b. 1872.
    [Elements of form & design in classic architecture]
    Form and design in classic architecture / Arthur Stratton.
        p. cm.
    Originally published: Elements of form & design in classic architecture.
London : B.T. Batsford, 1925.
    Includes index.
    ISBN 0-486-43405-2 (pbk.)
     1. Architecture, Classical. I. Title.

NA260.S77 2004
729'.0938—dc22

                                       2004043938

Manufactured in the United States of America
Dover Publications, Inc., 31 East 2nd Street, Mineola, N.Y. 11501

PREFACE

EXPERIENCE of teaching has convinced me of the need for a book dealing with elemental forms and first principles of design in classic architecture. Every architect should be familiar with the motives illustrated here, while to the student they are indispensable. As they are now—for the first time—conveniently arranged for reference and comparison, the task of teachers in making them known to the student should be rendered much less arduous than hitherto. It is not so much new teaching that is required as emphasis from a new viewpoint on old principles, and it is essential to lay such a foundation, as is here presented, upon which to build up a system of appropriate design. It is for this reason that I have persevered with what has proved to be a difficult undertaking. It would not, however, have been possible for me to carry it to completion had I not been so fortunate as to enlist the sympathetic help and encouragement of Professor A. E. Richardson, F.S.A., F.R.I.B.A., and Mr. Ronald P. Jones, M.A., F.R.I.B.A., almost from the time of its inception ten years ago. To many others I am indebted, especially for draughtsmanship, and my thanks are due in particular to Professor Leslie Wilkinson, F.R.I.B.A., Mr. Hector Corfiato, S.A.D.G., Miss Gertrude Leverkus, B.A., A.R.I.B.A., Mr. J. W. M. Harvey, B.A., A.R.I.B.A., and Mr. Arthur Ashdown, who have contributed the greater number of line drawings.

With the assistance of the librarians and officials at the British Museum, the Victoria and Albert Museum, South Kensington, the Royal Institute of British Architects and Sir John Soane's Museum, I have been able to select from the rare works in their keeping, while in Mr. Harry Batsford I have found a publisher who has generously placed his knowledge and unique collection of books, prints and drawings at my disposal. Plates XI, XIX and LIX (i) are from a series of water-colour drawings of English Domestic Architecture, by J. C. Buckler, belonging to Mrs. Mango, and are included by her kind permission. For the print of Carlton House (Plate XCV, i) I am indebted to Mr. Francis Edwards. In order to keep the volume within reasonable limits it has been necessary to restrict both the text and the scheme of the illustrations to their present scope, although much valuable material remains for future treatment in a further volume dealing with more advanced problems. But the purpose of this book will be amply fulfilled if it brings certain elements of form and design into such prominence that they can no longer be disregarded by anyone interested in the art of building.

ARTHUR STRATTON.

" Oriel,"
    Hampstead Way, N.W.,
        March, 1925.

CONTENTS

CONTENTS.

FOREWORD

THE purpose of this book is to supply an index to known forms of classic building and to present an analysis of elemental plans, sections and elevations arranged in a manner convenient for ready reference. While the author has found it expedient to base research on classic models, the book is not intended to encourage an extension of any particular type of stylistic building, neither does it lay stress on the furthering of tradition or the exploitation of any particular style. Its main object is rather to show, in the simplest way, the organic value of structural forms and to indicate how a building, whether large or small, depends for its ultimate expression on basic geometrical principles which are fundamental and constant.

Although it is possible for the experienced practitioner to enter upon the uncertain paths of adventure and from the depths of his knowledge to evolve novelty which may accord with the latest ideas, it is equally impossible for a beginner to neglect what has already been achieved. In the past, architects too often have selected motives from actual buildings or from authoritative books and have proceeded to fit them to new conditions, with the result that literal transcriptions have been made of historic models. This book has a more thorough purpose in view, for it aims at initiating all who are concerned with the design of buildings into first principles of arrangement irrespective of style, period or fashion, and its scope is deliberately limited to the most elementary of known forms.

The difficulties that beset a beginner, as well as a practising architect, when he is searching for a structural idea are many. Too often he essays a plan which cannot be developed in three dimensions, solely for want of sufficient knowledge of how such a theme can be carried to conclusion. Modern conditions call for up-to-date expression free from subservience to archæology, but this does not preclude the observance of principles which cannot be changed. Whether classic detail or any other stylistic articulation is used depends, however, upon the temperament of the individual designer. Most books of design attempt to condense the whole range of architectural achievement and to formulate theories which may or may not be of moment, but which in the process of time are bound to become obsolete. Besides being tedious and replete with irrelevant matter, such works tend to confuse the issue and to encourage an eclectic taste which is often pernicious in its results. Such faults have been only too common.

While a further volume dealing with more complex problems might with advantage be considered, it is felt that the scope of this book is more than sufficient to encourage adherence to rational theories. Much care has been expended upon the selection and arrangement of the examples illustrated : they should direct attention to the theory of vital building and enable all who see them to appreciate at a glance that completeness and unity of expression in fine structure which can only be developed from the ordered arrangement of plan and section. These are some of the purposes underlying the publication of the book and, if it is used rightly, it should have the result of enabling students and others to think for themselves, and in time to achieve that true quality which is never absent from the finest works of the past.

A. E. RICHARDSON.
Professor of Architecture in the University of London.

" To build . . .
    That is the noblest art of all the arts.
    Painting and sculpture are but images
    Are merely shadows cast by outward things
    On stone or canvas, having in themselves
    No separate existence.   Architecture
    Existing in itself, and not in seeming
    A something it is not, surpasses them
    As substance shadow."

PLATE II

COMPOSITIONS BY ITALIAN MASTERS

I. FROM AN UNSIGNED DRAWING IN THE LIBRARY OF THE ROYAL INSTITUTE OF BRITISH
ARCHITECTS, LONDON.

II. FROM AN UNSIGNED DRAWING IN THE LIBRARY, VICTORIA AND ALBERT MUSEUM,
LONDON.

INTRODUCTION.

"We are by nature observers, and thereby learners: that is our permanent state."—*Emerson.*

THE measure of success in the realm of design to which an architect will attain depends largely upon his recognition of elementary principles at the outset of his career and upon the selection of a right line of development for his future studies. Expression in architecture inevitably changes to meet the moods of passing fashion and taste, but the underlying principles remain constant. From earliest student days, the architect should be encouraged to appreciate geometrical form in building as the keynote to expression. In most countries classic architecture constitutes the bedrock of tradition, but all building—irrespective of style or period—that is worthy of the name of architecture responds to simple and elementary laws; observance of geometry underlies the grammar of the art and provides the basis of design.

Elementary forms often produce the most expressive results, for simplicity of plan suggests simplicity of section and elevation with corresponding dignity and restraint. When adequate to its purpose, the simplest expression is always the best, the qualities of simplicity and dignity being pre-eminently the attributes of greatness.

At the present time it is widely recognised that a study of first principles alone will give the designer a starting point from which he can proceed with confidence, and that a repertory of historical motives is essential as a basis upon which to formulate a standard whereby modern design can be gauged. In the past, masterpieces begat masterpieces, and constant reference to the finest examples of the art lays open to the designer an unfailing source of inspiration whence to evolve new aspects of beauty of his own. Reasoning, with reference to past achievement, has been the root of all fine architectural expression and character in buildings throughout the history of civilisation. While it must always be realised that peculiar conditions determine the geometrical arrangement in three dimensions of the component parts of any particular building, a mind guided to the right acceptance of the structural theory will the more readily evolve a building which has at least the merit of being architectural.

The present age is one of involved complexity, not only to the student but also to the practising architect. The sense of bewilderment tends to become more chaotic through lack of direction and the conflicting claims of new vogues

1

as one succeeds another.   To the uninitiated, the architectural outlook is obscured, while the tendency is unquestionably for the student to get confused by the overwhelming amount of detail bequeathed by the building arts during many centuries in different countries.   But a building or a monument appeals primarily by reason of its structural vitality.   " The architect's glory," wrote Sir Thomas Wootton, with real insight, " consists in the designment and idea of the work; his ambition should be to make the form triumph over the matter." There is, moreover, intuitively in the mind of every craftsman a perception of the beauty of form.   True insight into the qualities of a building is to be gained, not by enquiry about its historical associations, wealth of materials or variety of detail, but by investigation into the abstract form of its structure and the selection and grouping of the masses of which it is composed.   They are most readily approached through analysis of the elemental shapes upon which all buildings depend for expression, and experience has shown that specific forms and types of design lend themselves readily to analysis.

A century ago, the eminent French architect Durand* investigated certain elemental forms, and the knowledge which his researches made available has been applied—notably in France and America—to schemes of widely differing character.   New forms, however, have been evolved since Durand's time, and now with five hundred years of attainment and experience since the dawn of the Renaissance to look back upon, ampler opportunity offers itself, and it is possible to record not only antique models, but also other forms that are widely accepted as extending the theory.

A work of this description must of necessity emphasise the extraordinary similarity that prevails in building expression as interpreted by architects of different countries.   The greater part of the best European and American architecture is obviously based upon a common classic inheritance, deep-rooted in principles which have given to the world the supreme achievements of ancient Greece and Rome.   The awakening of the fifteenth century in Italy marked a new era of enlightenment and advance in the arts and, as a result of the appreciation of antique models, brought about a widespread return to the principles of design by which they are governed.   Consequently the culminating periods of Greek and Roman architecture have here been drawn upon as well as the whole range of matured Renaissance architecture in Europe.   Ideas developed in continuous sequence during many centuries are here collated and explicit statements formulated which give the designer the advantage of a clear index. Further, it has been realised that historical motives can be standardised for reference, and that themes acknowledged to be of superlative interest are capable of fresh development irrespective of style or scale.

* J. N. L. Durand.   *Précis des Leçons d'Architecture.*   2 vols.   Paris.   1802-9 and other editions.

The need for a clear analysis of the elements of design in the past is more than ever apparent. Such a work requires to be broad in its scope and definite in its purpose. Its scheme must embrace historical sequence; its theories must be elastic, the examples it illustrates must be inspiring. The fact that such examples have been employed in the past is no detriment to the repetition of the elemental idea. This in itself constitutes the law of design. With such ends in view, this work has been compiled, not only from actual buildings but also from the wider field of projected designs. The repositories of many countries have been searched, and from many sources material has been obtained to swell the number of useful examples, and at the same time to present the theories of architects who made history in England during the eighteenth and early nineteenth centuries. Many diagrams have been made especially to illustrate the geometrical basis upon which the buildings selected were designed. The main idea has been to demonstrate the structural principles which govern the particular series selected, and the book has been prepared primarily as a reference volume for the student as well as for the practising architect who may have occasion to deal with similar problems.

If architecture is to retain its place as chief among the kindred arts and to make any real progress in this country, it is certain that students must formulate their studies on first principles and base their essays in building on a clearly defined system. A definite purpose in teaching is most desirable, but before it can be pursued with advantage the student should be led to concentrate his attention on the essentials upon which expressive building depends.

In France, America and England it is now generally admitted that fundamental principles are not affected by limitations of time or space, and that purely local idiosyncrasies or conditions of climate or material do not annul the working of their laws. The elementary principles need to be assimilated by students and others, for to depart from them is to accept a " provincial " standard which in past decades has been productive of much commonplace building. A knowledge of the history of architecture and of the masterpieces which have survived reveals the fact that the men who stand out as masters of design have been content to study fundamental principles and to seek inspiration from precedent. Those, on the other hand, who were so eager for adventure that they discarded precedent—thinking to evolve all that seemed necessary out of their inner consciousness—have not gone far without realising that disregard of known laws has led them into uncertain and uncharted regions from which it would be wise to turn back and to dispense with their ill-judged originality. Energy spent in vain on a false road might, under better counsel, have been spent with success on a true one. The student, in particular, should be warned against trusting to his own judgment before he has laid in a store of material from which to enrich his ideas. Before being encouraged to " invent " he should, as far as practicable, be made familiar with the best simple structural forms and the most harmonious combinations of them that have already been produced.

The structural shapes, the proportions of the parts to one another and their relation to the whole constitute the elements of design in architecture as surely as in any other intellectual exercise. They are the most obvious and perceptible to the senses and so they are the most communicable, and from them most can be learned. It follows that an analysis of a number of accepted motives, selected from the works of past masters must give a foundation for future exercises, the aim of the student being to express himself clearly and to invest his designs with truth and grace, while avoiding immature attempts to " invent " on original lines. Nothing can come of nothing, but from the known advance can be made to the unknown. " Everything which is wrought with certainty is wrought upon some principle : if it is not, it cannot be repeated," was a famous saying of Sir Joshua Reynolds, than whom no teacher ever propounded saner precepts. The elementary forms of structure, evolved long ago, have been accepted as the basis of design for all time, and the measure of skill no less than the powers of invention acquired by the student will show themselves in the use he makes of them. To borrow an idea from an ancient building and to develop it is legitimate procedure. Such borrowing is a perpetual exercise of the inventive powers and is indispensable to the evolution of any art. Architectural development has depended upon it in the past, and without it ordered progress cannot be looked for in the future.

On the Plates in this book the elements of structure exhibiting classic design and composition are graphically analysed and arranged in geometrical sequence. With some exceptions, the illustrations do not represent actual buildings drawn to the exact scale of the originals : on the contrary, they show types adopted from the antique and developed at various periods. The drawings indicate the elements of the design of innumerable buildings, arranged with due regard to their dimensions, in such a way as to facilitate comparison. The motives, grouped according to their plan form, cover a wide range of design extending from those of extreme simplicity and modest dimensions to those suitable for a magnificent scale, but no attempt has been made to suggest finality of composition. These simple plan forms are capable of endless development, and every student should be familiar with them and should obtain a certain mastery over their relation to section and elevation before attempting to solve more difficult problems, for they underlie the design of many compositions which at first sight appear to be complex. The designs here drawn and described are not intended to pre-determine the character of particular types of buildings, nor it is supposed that they will influence planning otherwise than by showing the correct placing of attributes and by ensuring sympathetic relation of parts, without which architecture lacks true quality. Hitherto, it has not been generally realised in this country that design in building is primarily concerned with the plan, and that the highest architectural expression can be found only in a building that is rhythmically composed in plan, section and elevation.

A work of art must possess unity. It is through a symmetrical arrangement that a work of architecture reveals itself as an organic unit and as the expression of a central thought. The law of balance calls for a symmetrical disposition of the elements, whether of plan or of elevation, grouped about axial lines. In order to appreciate the correct setting-out of a plan and the importance of vistas, the student must gain a knowledge of the fundamental principles of planning, and this will strengthen his theories of logical construction, inasmuch as it ensures a just proportion and cohesion between solids and voids and between the areas of supports and the areas enclosed. Perfection in plan is indispensable to perfection in architectural expression.

A geometrical basis should govern all design, for geometrical forms are naturally more pleasing than irregular figures. The circle, the square and the rectangle being elemental are of most frequent occurrence. Certain accepted methods of treating simple circular, polygonal, square and rectangular plans, both internally and externally, cannot be ignored and familiarity with them, derived from a study of the finest works of all times and all countries affords a broad foundation on which to base further solutions. Rectangular figures of varying proportions and such regular polygonal, segmental and elliptical figures as concern the architect, give the elemental plan forms of buildings, all of which in the past have been treated architecturally, either alone or in combination, and certain methods of enclosing, covering and lighting specific forms have been established by long usage.

The principles governing the design of structures that consist in plan of one simple geometrical form only must especially be brought to the notice of the student, and many of the Plates that follow are concerned with these. But the majority of buildings—specially those erected under modern conditions—not being restricted to a single use, consist of more than one apartment and become more complex with the number of apartments provided and the variety of uses which they serve. Thus, buildings consist, not only of apartments, but also of approaches to them through porticoes, porches and vestibules, and of communications between the apartments disposed horizontally by means of halls, ante-rooms, covered ways and corridors, and vertically by means of steps and staircases, both external and internal. These units of which buildings of more than one storey in height are composed should be studied individually with a view to ascertaining not only the most logical and the most comely method of covering appropriate to any given plan form, but also the most suitable proportion of height to breadth, and above all the most effective means of admitting light. Further, their sub-division, horizontally by piers and columns and vertically by galleries, calls for rare skill on the part of designer as well as reliance upon accepted models.

It is obvious that the different units of which buildings are composed may be placed, not only side by side but also over one another. To an experienced designer, composing a building of more than one storey in height, these two aspects of composition present themselves simultaneously, but in order to render the study less difficult it is advisable at first to consider them separately. There are thus two main kinds of disposition which the architect is constantly called upon to handle : the horizontal, represented by the plan, and the vertical represented by the section and elevation. The arrangement of staircases in rectangular and other spaces should certainly be investigated by the student before attempting the design of buildings containing more than one principal floor.

The numerous rectangular and curved forms, used alone or in combination, which appear in the plans of various kinds of apartments and their connections—considered in relation to the section most appropriate to each—constitute the elements of composition as far as the interiors of buildings are concerned. As it is not possible to compose without a knowledge of the elements constituting a design, it follows that a thorough grasp of the primary forms should be gained before proceeding to the elaboration of detail or to the design of a building made up of many parts. " So in architecture," Inigo Jones wrote in 1614, " one must first study the parts as Loggias, Entrances, Halls, Chambers, Stairs . . . and then adorn them."

In the design of the exterior, precedent will still be the surest safeguard for the student. The arrangement of columns in porticoes, peristyles, screens and simple colonnades ; of porches recessed and projecting, of pediments and attics are all represented in the series of Plates which follow. Pavilions, loggias, and simple façades—not exceeding two principal storeys in height and in many instances dependent for their effect upon the correct spacing and grouping of window openings—are also well represented and should prove a ready source of reference. There is no limit to the number and variety of arrangements that may be evolved, and the student should always be seeking fresh dispositions beautiful in themselves. But the laws of composition which have been evolved must never be ignored, nor the results which they have brought about be overlooked. Rhythm and proportion are nebulous terms that cannot be profitably described and analysed. Without the qualities they impart, however, no work of architecture can claim to be of real and lasting importance.

All the buildings and motives graphically presented on the Plates in this book are shown in their simplest aspect, free from confusing detail, so that the main lines of the various schemes may be understood at a glance. It is left to the student to clothe them and to supply accessories which give richness of detail and colour contrasts, bearing in mind that applied ornament is not essential to fine architecture, whereas rigorous attention to the actual form of a structure is of vital importance. It may be broadly asserted that in the initial stage of a design, questions of detail, ornament, sculpture and colour do not necessarily affect the main disposition.

It has been found possible to touch little more than the fringe of this fascinating and inexhaustible subject. To include the whole range of design and composition within the limits of a single volume is impracticable, and to attempt it would defeat the end to which this work is directed. It has, for instance, been thought advisable to eliminate all designs depending for their expression upon the introduction of columns that do not perform their true function as weight-bearing members, while compositions culminating in the dome as an external feature, where the external dome bears no direct relation to the internal domical covering—as at St. Paul's Cathedral, London, and the Panthéon, Paris —properly belong to a more advanced system than can be dealt with here. But the motives presented cover a field wide enough to illustrate the principles of design governing structure in all its elemental forms, principles which do not alter with the size of a building or a monument, although they vary in application according to the conditions affecting the solution of the more complex problems which confront the practising architect.

Research into the qualities of natural and reconstructed materials and acceptance of modern conditions have proved of inestimable value and have enabled problems to be solved satisfactorily in recent times while avoiding such marked solidity of construction as was inevitable in the past. Such advanced methods rightly have their claims at the present day, but the architectural theory is by no means affected other than in an economical direction.

There is reason to hope that if students and others are directed to the models laid before them in this book, and to the sources from which they are drawn, the vital qualities of building—which were partially overshadowed, at least in England, during the experimental years of the nineteenth century—may be recovered and universally recognised. With a clear insight into the methods and arrangement of structure which have been understood and practised by a long succession of masters, and with a knowledge of modern needs and materials, progress in the right direction may be anticipated with confidence.

GENERAL REFERENCE BOOKS.

As so large a proportion of the standard books in various European languages that have been consulted are rare and costly, no useful purpose would be served by enumerating them all here. In fact, this book claims to present many motives which are now well known, but the original sources of which are buried in ponderous volumes no longer accessible to the student and general reader. The list of standard works given at the end of the text to most of the Series have therefore been reduced to a working minimum, and they are intended to guide the student in his endeavours to supplement the elements of form and design illustrated, and in no way to indicate the field of research covered by the author.

Blondel, J. F. *Cours d'Architecture.* 1771-7.

Bühlmann, J. *Die Architektur des Classischen Altertums und der Renaissance.* 1893.

Canina, L. *L'Architettura Antica.* 1839-44.

Cloquet, L. *Traité d'Architecture.* 1898-1901.

D'Espouy, H. *Fragments de l'Architecture Antique.* 1896-1923.

D'Espouy, H., et Seure, G. *Monuments Antiques.* 1915.

Durand, J. N. L. *Précis des Leçons d'Architecture.* 1802-9.

Durand, J. N. L., et Legrand, J. G. *Recueil et Paralléle des Edifices de tout genre Anciens et Modernes.* 1842.

Gourlier. *Choix d'Edifices Publics Projetés et Construits en France Depuis le Commencement du XIXme Siècle.* 1825-36.

Klenze, Leo von. *Sammlung Architektonischer Entwürfe.* 1830-50.

Letarouilly, P. M. *Les Edifices de Rome Moderne.* 1868-74.

Les Médailles des Concours d'Architecture de l'Ecole Nationale des Beaux Arts à Paris. 1897 and in progress.

Neufforge, J. F. *Recueil Elémentaire d'Architecture.* 1757-68.

ON DESIGN AND COMPOSITION.

Curtis, N. C. *Architectural Composition.* 1923.

Guadet, J. *Eléments et Theorie de l'Architecture.* 1904.

Gromort, G. *Choix d'Eléments Empruntés à l'Architecture Classique.* 1920.

Robinson, J. B. *Architectural Composition.* 1908.

Robertson, Howard. *The Principles of Architectural Composition.* 1924.

Van Pelt, J. V. *The Essentials of Composition as Applied to Art.* 1913.

ORIGINAL DRAWINGS AND DESIGNS.

The collections at the British Museum, Victoria and Albert Museum, Sir John Soane's Museum and the Royal Institute of British Architects have been freely drawn upon in addition to designs and sketches by Joseph Bonomi, J. C. Buckler, Professor C. R. Cockerell and other artists in private collections.

I

CIRCULAR PLANS.

PLATES III TO X.

THE circle gives one of the elemental plan forms, and it has always figured prominently in design by reason of the beauty of its curve and the endless variety which it introduces into a scheme. The theory underlying the application of the circle has been developed through the centuries in buildings of many types, ranging from small isolated structures of a commemorative nature to those of considerable size suitable for ecclesiastical and secular purposes.

The circular plan is generally accompanied by a domical section, for the dome has from early times been accepted as its logical covering because it gives the best vertical expression to the horizontal disposition. The support for a dome over a circular plan is readily obtained, and its arrangement so as to produce the most satisfactory result as seen from the interior has been one of the chief aims of builders at all times. Various arrangements of coffering have been devised by recessing panels within horizontal and vertical ribs, and when an unbroken surface for mosaic or colour decoration has not been required, one of the many varieties of coffering has invariably been used to give architectural expression to the concave surface. The properties of domical construction allow of an opening being left at the top, and advantage has been taken of this to let in light where it can be most impressively admitted through a circular " eye."

Externally many variations are permissible : the domical form may be visible, following the curve of the inner covering as nearly as permitted by the demands of sound construction. The lower part of the dome is sometimes masked by a vertical wall above which a conical roof conceals the curve of the dome completely, or the segment of the curve remaining above the vertical surface may be exposed. When it is desired to emphasise the dome externally and to admit light just beneath its base instead of at its summit, the dome may be raised on a vertical wall or " drum." Sections and elevations of these dispositions will be found in this series of Plates, and the theory of the setting-out of domes over rectangular sub-structures by means of " pendentives " is illustrated on Plate XII.

The impossibility of producing satisfactory expression both internally and externally from the use of a single domical covering is apparent in the domed buildings of the ancients, but it was left to the architects of the Renaissance in Italy, France and eventually in England to construct the double and triple coverings which, in their hands, were productive of such magnificent results. But compositions culminating in domes, the inner and outer coverings of which are at different levels, do not come within the scope of this book as they belong to the more complex systems.

The diagrams on the following Plates have been arranged with regard to the approximate diameter of the dome most suitable for the type of plan and section shown, and they provide a basis for further development when the student has mastered the elementary principles which they illustrate.

Plates III and IV.—These illustrate the simplest types of circular plan with domical coverings, taken from authoritative examples. On Plate III, Nos. I, II and III, and Plate IV, No. I, are shown open circular structures which offer suggestions for garden pavilions, shelters for statuary, or fountains. No. IV has often been used to enclose a wellhead, but both this and No. V readily suggest the small private mausoleum or cenotaph.

Plate V.—The circular plan is shown here with an external peristyle, a favourite disposition at all periods, the domical covering not being necessarily expressed externally, as in No. I. The motives given in Nos. I, II and III, and in the perspective sketch (Fig. 1), are suitable for any structure of small size which is primarily monumental and intended to serve a single use, such as a mausoleum or memorial chapel. The example from Castle Howard, Yorkshire, Plate IV, No. II, is a well-known instance introducing a dignified arrangement of external steps. In No. III the dome is raised on a high " drum " pierced with windows, but light is still admitted through a central " eye " in the dome. The type shown in No. IV originated at Baalbec, Syria, and has been sparingly followed : the entablature breaking back from the columns of the peristyle to the circular wall in a series of curves gives a striking play of line, but as it lacks repose it is more suitable for a garden feature—as used by Sir William Chambers at Kew Gardens—than for a memorial of any kind. The lower plan, No. V, shows how the peristyle may be interrupted and a rectangular portico added to steady the effect of so many curving lines.

Plate VI.—These larger circular structures with sub-motives are especially suitable for memorial chapels and mausoleums. They are complete in themselves, but they can be adapted to form dominating features in a variety of compositions.

Plate VII.—The combination of the circle with the square shown in Nos. I, II and III was developed from a Roman type. This is the Chapelle Expiatoire at Paris and it is essentially in the nature of a memorial. Further applications of this theory are discussed and illustrated in Series II. The large circular motives shown on this Plate are applicable to buildings in isolated positions for such uses as national pantheons. In Nos. IV and V an external peristyle is provided, while in Nos. VI and VII the ambulatory is formed by a ring of internal columns. The building shown in Nos. VIII, IX and X belongs to the type of the Pantheon,

FIG. 1.—ISOLATED BUILDING ON A CIRCULAR PLAN WITH PERISTYLE.

Rome, which in almost every country figures as a motive for isolated domed buildings on the largest scale.

Plate VIII.—These circular motives are taken from plans which are set out with a view to obtaining internal vistas along axial lines, and they are suitable for points of interest in the arrangement of interiors. In such cases the domical covering is not necessarily expressed externally and the circular plan is enclosed within walls which become square so as to conform with the adjacent rooms. No. I is the simplest type, with light admitted through an " eye " at the crown of a coffered dome : in No. II pairs of columns are attached to the walls and carry an entablature, while in No. III columns stand free in front of recesses alternating with wide piers, producing an effective arrangement. In some cases it is necessary to continue the circular plan through two or more storeys, by means of a gallery or galleries, leaving a circular " well " in the centre. In No. IV the simplest way of achieving this is represented, and in No. V a circular range of columns is disposed on two floors, carrying a domical covering over the central " well " only.

Plates IX and X.—Further developments of the circular plan on a large scale are given here with interest centering in the interior treatment of the dome as part of a large conception. Several types of plan have been selected for illustration, but many other variations are possible. In Nos. I and II the dome would not be expressed as a dominating external feature. These and the interior perspective view on Plate IX are taken from the Museum at Berlin. It will be seen that a highly decorative effect results from this studied arrangement of an internal peristyle and the contrast of curves at different levels. In Nos. III, IV and V the dominant motive appears both internally and externally. These have been selected to show the development of the circular plan on lines of rich simplicity. Attention has been given to circulation and direct access, the staircases and other features being introduced as external steadying features without which no circular building of large scale can be regarded as entirely satisfactory. In No. IV double columns on radial lines separate the circular hall from the ambulatory and these columns are expressed externally by pilasters directly radial on plan. The steadying features in this case consist of a tetrastyle portico connected to the

FIG. 2.—RADCLIFFE LIBRARY, OXFORD.
(*See also Plate X, No. V.*)

external wall of the rotunda, and a square bay containing a semi-circular recess as a posterior feature. No. V shows a circular plan, consisting of eight bays internally, one of which is allocated to the entrance and staircase. The feature of the plan is the distribution of the internal composite piers. The gallery or upper ambulatory forms a prominent feature of the interior, additional height being given by an arcade supporting the dome. Externally the basement storey assumes a polygonal form of sixteen bays and the fine composition obtained by James Gibbs is suggested in the sketch reproduced in Fig. 2.

REFERENCE BOOKS.

Bolton, Arthur T. *The Works of Sir John Soane.* 1924.
D'Espouy, H. *Fragments de l'Architecture Antique.* 1896-1923.
Gibbs, James. *Bibliotheca Radcliviana.* 1747.
Gourlier. *Choix d'Edifices Publics.* 1825-36.
Isabelle, C. E. *Les Edifices Circulaires.* 1855.
Normand, J. L. *Monuments Funéraires de Paris.* 1847.
Peyre, M. J. *Œuvres d'Architecture.* 1765.
Schinkel, C. F. *Sammlung Architectonischer Entwürfe.* 1836.

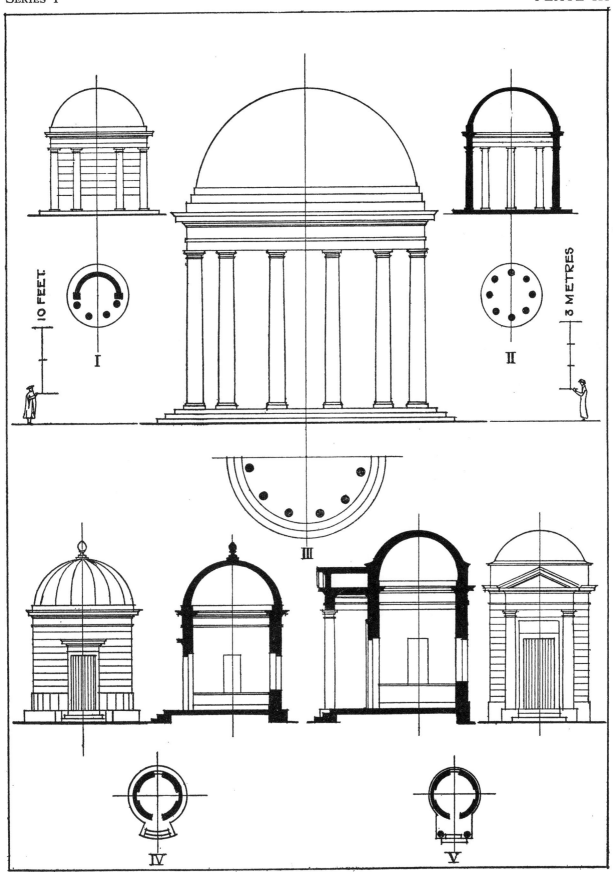

CIRCULAR PLANS.

I-V. GENERAL TYPES OF SMALL CIRCULAR FEATURES BASED ON AUTHENTIC EXAMPLES.

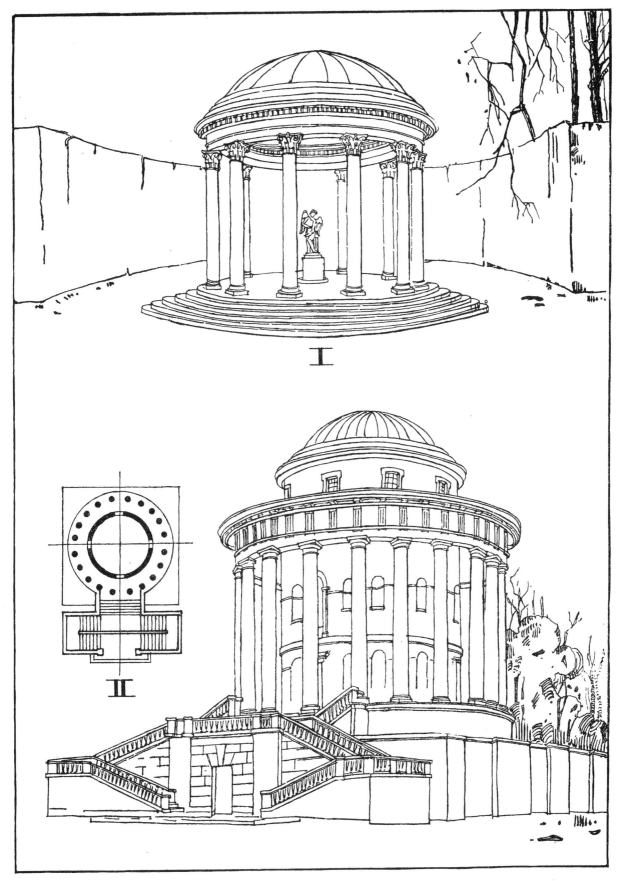

CIRCULAR PLANS.

I· SIMPLE DOMED STRUCTURE WITH OPEN RING OF COLUMNS.   EXAMPLE: TEMPLE DE L'AMOUR AT VERSAILLES,
DESIGNED BY MIQUE.
II. CIRCULAR DOMED CELL WITH PERISTYLE ON HIGH PODIUM WITH EXTERNAL STAIRCASE.   EXAMPLE: THE MAUSOLEUM,
CASTLE HOWARD, YORKSHIRE, DESIGNED BY NICHOLAS HAWKSMOOR.

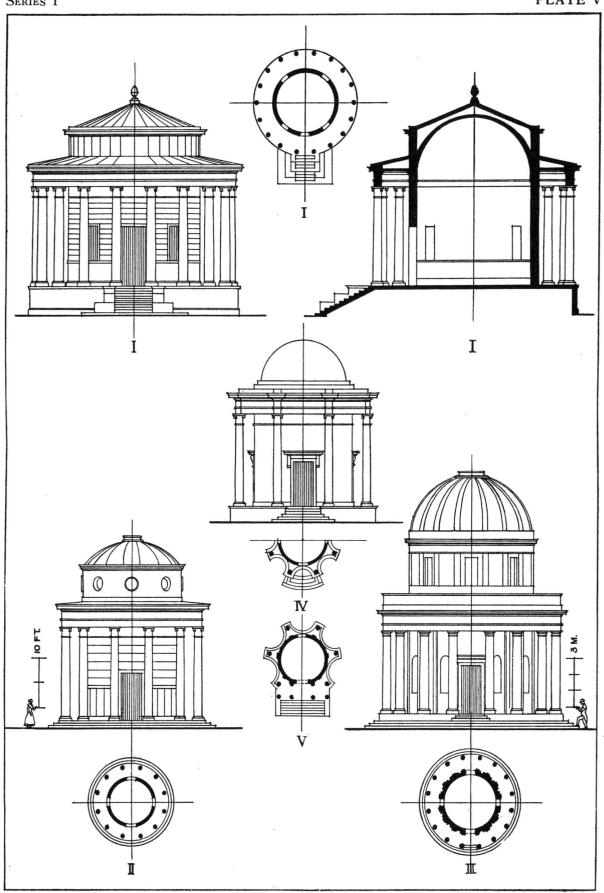

CIRCULAR PERIPTERAL PLANS WITH DOMICAL COVERINGS

I.   BASED ON TEMPLE OF VESTA AT TIVOLI.   IV.   BASED ON TEMPLE OF VENUS AT BAALBEC.
II. GENERAL TYPE, ENGLISH EIGHTEENTH CENTURY.   V.   THE SAME, SHOWING ADJUSTMENT OF A PORTICO.
III. BASED ON THE " TEMPIETTO," ROME, DESIGNED BY BRAMANTE.

PLATE VI

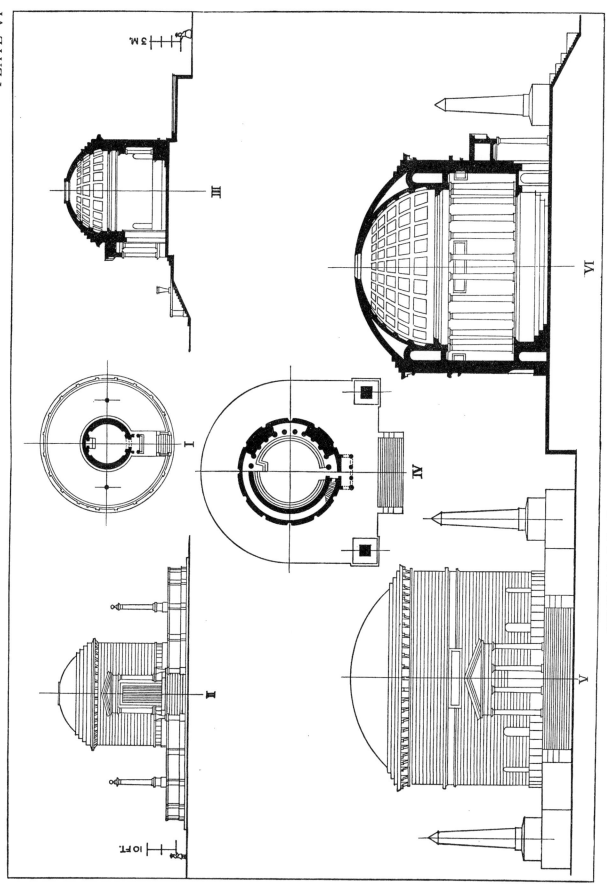

CIRCULAR DOMED BUILDINGS WITH SUB-MOTIVES.

I-III. BASED ON MONUMENT AT ORANGE, FRANCE, DESIGNED BY CARISTIL.
IV-VI. BASED ON A DESIGN BY M. J. PEYRE.

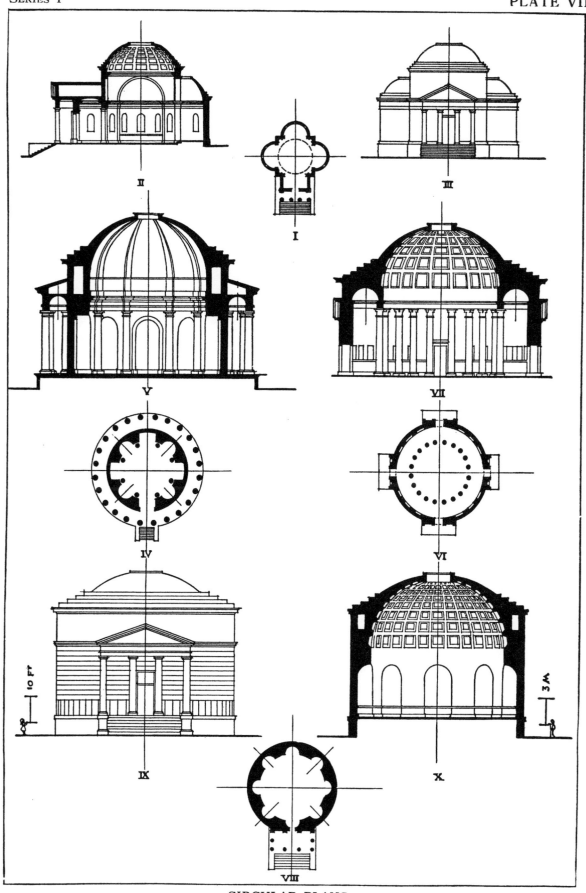

CIRCULAR PLANS.

I-III.   BASED ON THE CHAPELLE EXPIATOIRE, PARIS, DESIGNED BY PERCIER AND FONTAINE.
IV-V   CIRCULAR DOMED BUILDING WITH EXTERNAL AMBULATORY.
VI-VII.   CIRCULAR DOMED BUILDING WITH INTERNAL AMBULATORY.
VIII-X   PANTHEON TYPE WITH INTERNAL NICHES.

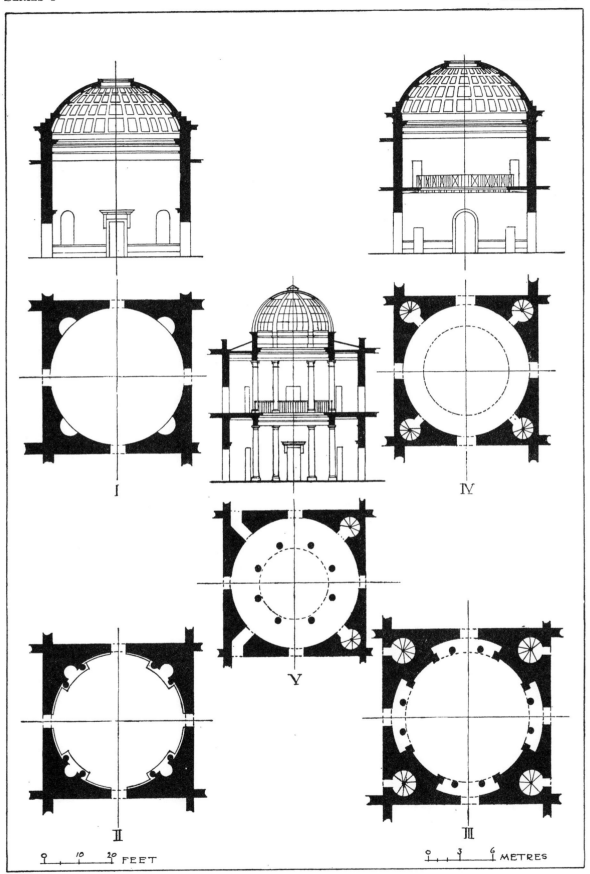

CIRCULAR PLANS DISPOSED FOR INTERNAL EFFECT

I-III. GENERAL TYPES.   IV. TWO-STORIED INTERIOR WITH GALLERY.
        V. TWO-STORIED INTERIOR WITH SUPER-IMPOSED ORDERS, BASED ON A DESIGN BY JAMES PAINE.

CIRCULAR INTERIOR WITH AMBULATORY

ROTUNDA IN THE MUSEUM, BERLIN, DESIGNED BY C. F. SCHINKEL.
(See Plate X, Nos. I and II for plan and section)

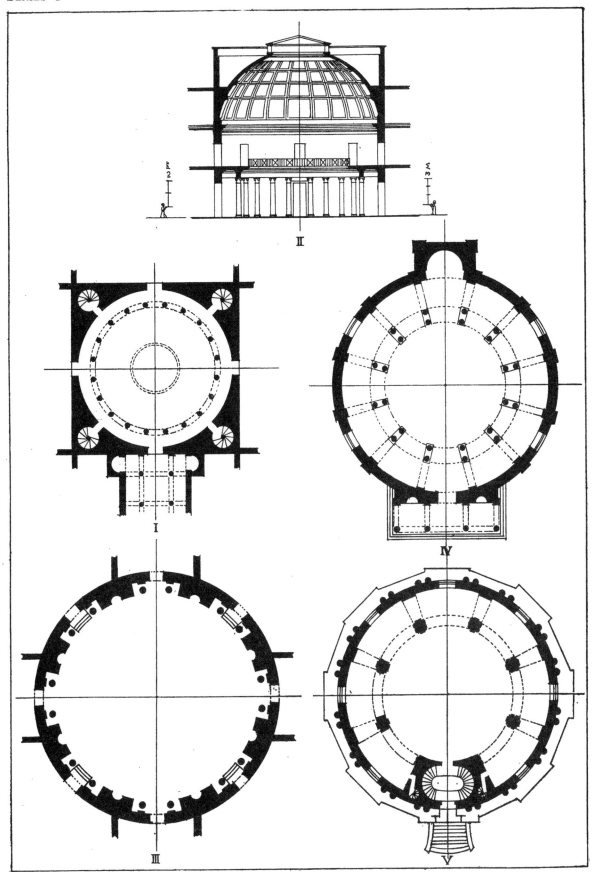

CIRCULAR PLANS OF LARGE DIMENSIONS

I–II   BASED ON THE ROTUNDA IN THE MUSEUM, BERLIN, DESIGNED BY C. F. SCHINKEL.

III.   BASED ON "FOUR COURTS," DUBLIN, DESIGNED BY JAMES GANDON.

IV   GENERAL TYPE   EXAMPLE: STA. COSTANZA, ROME.

V.   BASED ON THE RADCLIFFE LIBRARY, OXFORD, DESIGNED BY JAMES GIBBS.

II

CIRCULAR AND RECTANGULAR FORMS UNITED.

PLATES XI TO XIV.

PLANS combining circular with rectangular forms have been widely used in the past and they lend themselves to many problems arising in modern practice. It is only possible here to deal with simple examples and to indicate methods of uniting the two elements which experience will enable the student to elaborate.

The combination of the square and the circle played an important part in English architecture of the late eighteenth century, when examples were evolved in which the circular feature dominates both horizontally and vertically, forming an architectural *ensemble* generally enriched with a peristyle. The works of the Brothers Adam, Sir William Chambers, the Wyatts and Sir John Soane show the practice that prevailed from about 1760 to 1820. Many compositions of this period are most attractive. Fanciful dispositions were developed in all countries during the Renaissance period which prove the desire felt by designers to achieve novelty within certain limitations. Both the circle and the ellipse have been used in planning at all periods to produce contrasts in architectural schemes. In France, during the closing years of the eighteenth century and during the régime of the Empire, this treatment was much favoured by French architects, while new theories were freely evolved at this period.

The circle with appendages is rarely found in large buildings : in the past it was reserved for comparatively small works, such as orangeries and pavilions. The circle when adopted as an integral feature of buildings on a large scale invariably governs the plan formation and, except in those cases where it is domed, it is not generally expressed externally. The principle of combining the circle with the square having been grasped, the theory is open to innumerable interpretations. The circle and the square can be used as primary motives in the external expression of buildings of immense size, provided that the character of the building allows of this arrangement. The student who has developed his knowledge of buildings designed on geometrical principles will readily understand the possibilities of further combinations.

Plates XI and XII.—These show the circular plan used over a square substructure, a combination of two elemental plan forms in a vertical direction of the first importance, developed originally by Byzantine dome builders. Accepted in all countries throughout the Renaissance period, this application of

27

geometry to the solution of a structural problem frequently occurs in modern buildings. The introduction of a domical covering gives expression to a plan by determining a climax in internal perspective, and it may also be relied upon to ensure that an important junction appears dominant.

On Plate XII the diagrams Nos. I to VI show alternative solutions of the domical problem, but plan No. I applies to all of them. The diagrams Nos. VII, VIII and IX illustrate the theory of the " pendentive." It is a property of the hemisphere that when cut by true planes, circles or segments of circles will be formed. If cut by four vertical planes, representing four supporting arches forming an inscribed square on plan, as shown in No. VII, the curves of four semi-circular arches will be produced, and the portions remaining at the four angles will constitute the pendentives. Thus the full semi-circle occurs only on the diagonal section, and a cross section gives a segment as seen in Nos. II and V. If the hemisphere is also cut horizontally at the level of the crown of the arches, nothing will remain of it beyond the four pendentives which, starting from the four angles of a square, form a circle on plan directly they unite. Upon this circle, once obtained, it is perfectly easy to place another hemisphere and to obtain a compound dome, as shown in No. VIII. The curve of the dome and of its pendentives is then no longer continuous, since the radius of the former is equal to half the side of the square instead of half the diagonal : the one, in fact, is invariably marked off from the other by a cornice or a series of mouldings, as in No. IV. The dome, instead of being placed directly upon the pendentives can now be raised above them upon a cylindrical wall or " drum " of the required height, as in Nos. III and VI. This device facilitates the admission of light without cutting into and weakening the dome about its springing where strength is most required, and the additional height so gained gives a greater prominence to the external design of the domical covering. In the finest examples, prior to this development, the dome though majestic and all sufficient internally had shown externally as little more than an excrescence.

Plate XIII.—This shows circular and rectangular plan forms united in a building of three principal parts with connecting links. Such a building suggests a motive for orangeries, public shelters in parks or on the esplanades of watering places. The scheme also lends itself to the requirements of a sculpture gallery in the open or a memorial containing mural tablets.

Plate XIV.—This shows five varieties of the circular plan form united with the rectangle. Based on the design of the small eighteenth century casino, they have been selected on account of the precise adjustment of their parts and the variety of architectural contrasts which result. Although the casino is no longer considered in relation to a large country house, its features might well be embodied in the design of pleasure buildings for public use.

THE DOME OVER A SQUARE SUBSTRUCTURE

(Similar to plan on Plate XII)

THE CHAPEL, DODINGTON, GLOUCESTERSHIRE, DESIGNED BY JAMES WYATT.

FROM A SKETCH BY J. C. BUCKLER.

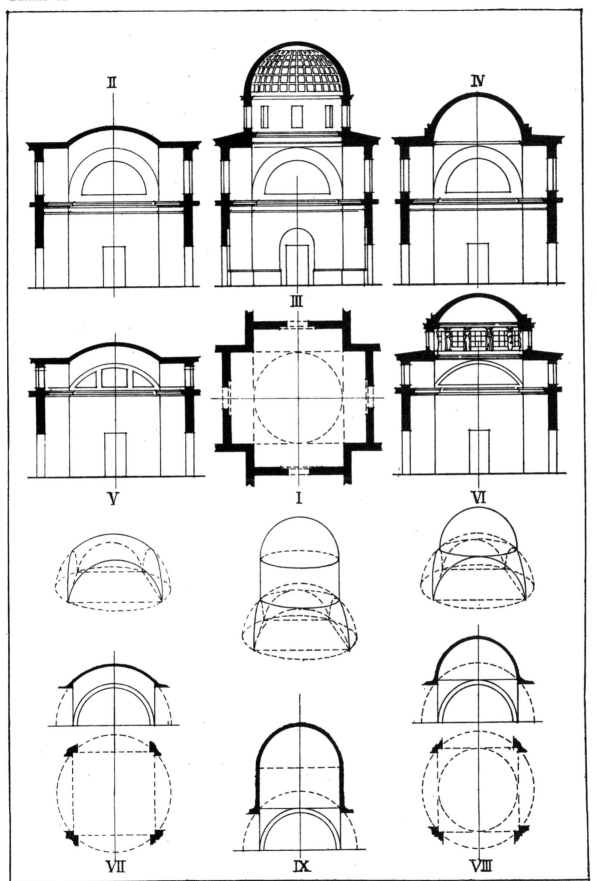

SQUARE FORMS WITH DOMICAL COVERINGS

SHOWING THE ADJUSTMENT OF THE DOME, WHICH IS CIRCULAR ON PLAN, TO THE SUBSTRUCTURE, WHICH IS SQUARE, BY MEANS OF
" PENDENTIVES."

PLATE XIII

I

II

III

3M

10 FT

PLAN SHOWING CIRCULAR AND RECTANGULAR FORMS UNITED

I-III. PLAN, ELEVATION AND PERSPECTIVE, BASED ON A DESIGN BY C. F. SCHINKEL.

PLATE XIV

PLANS SHOWING CIRCULAR AND RECTANGULAR FORMS UNITED

I-V. BASED ON ORIGINAL STUDIES BY SIR WILLIAM CHAMBERS IN THE VICTORIA AND ALBERT MUSEUM, LONDON.

III

SQUARE PLANS.

PLATES XV TO XVIII.

AMONG the elemental plan forms which are in constant use, the square offers unlimited scope for treatment, ranging from isolated buildings of small dimensions to those of great size containing a geometrical patterning made up of sub-divisions both rectangular and circular. It is impossible to describe in detail the many uses to which the square form can be adapted, for it figures in buildings of every period and has been developed in a variety of ways. It would not be too much to say that the square and circular plan forms are the determining factors in design, and modern investigation of historic examples proves that the square has been taken as the unit in planning and design generally.

It is the object of the following series of Plates to give some of the chief dispositions accompanying the simple square plan, formed not only by enclosing walls but also by columns, as well as by walls in conjunction with columns. Such isolated structures, complete in themselves and generally of small size (Fig. 3), offer a wide range for design : in the larger examples, the square plan occurs in conjunction with subsidiary and sympathetic features showing the development from simplicity to complexity.

The square is frequently used as an interior motive in a composition made up of many parts and not necessarily expressed externally, and several ways of treating it are illustrated. It must be borne in mind that the square is the most difficult form for direct architectural treatment and one that calls for a sound knowledge of geometry, for any departure from the simplicity of the square as an elemental plan form involves the introduction of smaller units in sympathetic consonance with the containing square. Buildings square in plan, when they are of simple type, generally correspond to the square in height, thus enclosing a space which approximates in its three dimensions to the cube, while the double cube is accepted as a satisfactory disposition of length and width to height under almost any circumstances.

The illustrations show a variety of treatments mostly based upon actual examples, in which the design of external frontispieces, with or without colonnades, and internal vaults, domes and ceilings indicates the application of the unit and deals with the elements of support and covering. The exterior design of small square features generally resolves itself into the expression of pediments, pyramidal roofs or curved and sloping coverings. Sometimes the pediment is lifted to accommodate a semi-circular lunette or a parapet is introduced to mask a flat roof.

The square apartment can be covered with either a flat ceiling, cove, cross vaulting or a dome, and examples of all of these are given, but they are not to be looked upon as exhausting the possible ways of covering a square, for at the beginning of the nineteenth century types of " umbrella " ceilings were designed by Sir John Soane and other architects of his school : these, however, are chiefly remarkable for their ingenuity.

Occasionally problems arise in which two or more storeys have to be dealt with internally, leaving a central open " well " : examples of such galleried arrangements are shown on Plate XVIII. The square plan, sub-divided internally and carrying a clerestorey with a flat or coved ceiling is useful from both utilitarian and artistic standpoints. This arrangement can be extended by the inclusion of a flat dome or a cove above the clerestorey.

FIG. 3.   SQUARE TOLL-HOUSE AT
REMOULINS, FRANCE.

Plate XV.—The types shown in Nos. I and II suggest small features for the furnishing of streets, such as kiosks, shelters and ticket offices : they might also be used for lodges in certain positions. Nos. III and VI are suitable either for garden pavilions or for public shelters, while Nos. IV and V show the architectural treatment of a lodge either at the entrance to a park or in connection with a pleasure garden. In Nos. VII, VIII and IX are given types which are useful for terminating large enclosing screens such as complete the courtyards of public and other buildings where it is necessary for a keeper or a sentry to have a place of retirement.

Plate XVI.—These schemes are especially appropriate where it is desired to produce interior architectural effect in a hall or vestibule of small dimensions which forms the meeting point of two or more suites of rooms. In No. I such an apartment is shown with a saucer dome carried on pendentives : a circular entablature intervenes between the pendentives and the dome. No. II shows the simplest treatment for a square apartment either with a flat ceiling and cornice as shown, or with a regular entablature proportioned to the height of the room. In No. III the proportion of a cube is followed with the introduction of a cove one quarter to one-fifth of the total height : this produces a square panel in the centre of the ceiling and emphasises the shape of the apartment. No. IV shows a square apartment ceiled with true cross vaults, thereby admitting light on four sides at an upper level. In marked contrast to this is the " cloister vault " or high coved ceiling shown in No. V, which has concave groins and leaves a square panel in the centre. No. VI shows how a square can be developed into an octagon at a higher level by means of semi-vaults meeting at the points of a central octagonal panel. In No. VII is seen a type common to Italian practice, in which the Order is omitted and a geometrical disposition of groined coves supports a flat ceiling in the centre.

Plate XVII.—Further arrangements of square apartments which form points of interest in extensive plans are given in Nos. I and II on this Plate. In both schemes an inner square is formed by means of four detached columns carrying entablatures, the small square spaces in the angles having flat ceilings at the cornice level, and the side spaces being covered with barrel vaults allowing of lunettes on all four sides. But different treatments are adopted over the central areas : in No. I cross vaults complete the scheme, while in No. II pendentives are introduced to carry a saucer dome. In Nos. III and IV the square plan is treated not so much as a unit of scenic interest as a large apartment in which the maximum floor space is a necessity and in which it is desired to present interest and contrast in the ceiling. These plans have been selected from those evolved by Sir Christopher Wren for some of his churches in the City of London : they should be studied carefully as outstanding examples of geometric and perspective skill. No. III excels through its forceful simplicity as well as its ingenuity and variety. The Order is omitted and by means of a series of pendentives springing from corbels, a large saucer dome is carried encircling the supports and contrasting with the square plan. Such an arrangement increases the apparent size of an apartment and produces an impressive effect. No. IV shows a square apartment in which an attached Order is introduced : this in turn carries an entablature which is taken across the angles and forms an octagon supporting an octagonal vaulted ceiling.

Plate XVIII.—The examples given on this Plate have been selected on account of their value as suggestions for internal architectural effect at certain points of plans and in relation to groups of corridors and apartments : they have little value as isolated units for public accommodation. No. I shows a square hall with a gallery carried on consoles and ceiled by means of a cove and a flat ceiling : the proportion of width to height approximates to the cube and the arrangement is based on the best practice of English eighteenth century designers. No. II shows a development of a containing square with grouped columns geometrically disposed in order to reduce the central space which is expressed vertically as a clerestorey and lighted by lunettes. This example demands a flat ceiling.   The design given in Nos. III and IV represents a containing square with two galleries open to a central " well," the lower carried on columns and the upper on consoles; lighting is obtained through lunettes on two sides.   This type offers suggestions for connecting features in a plan where continuity of corridors leading to groups of apartments has to be considered at two upper levels and attention paid to lighting and scenic effects.   Nos. V and VI show variations of treatment applicable to the same plan and suitable for halls of one storey in height, No. V being lighted by means of clerestorey windows, and No. VI through a central top light.

FIG. 4.   INTERIOR OF THE PUBLIC LIBRARY, PLYMOUTH, DESIGNED BY JOHN FOULSTON.

PLATE XV

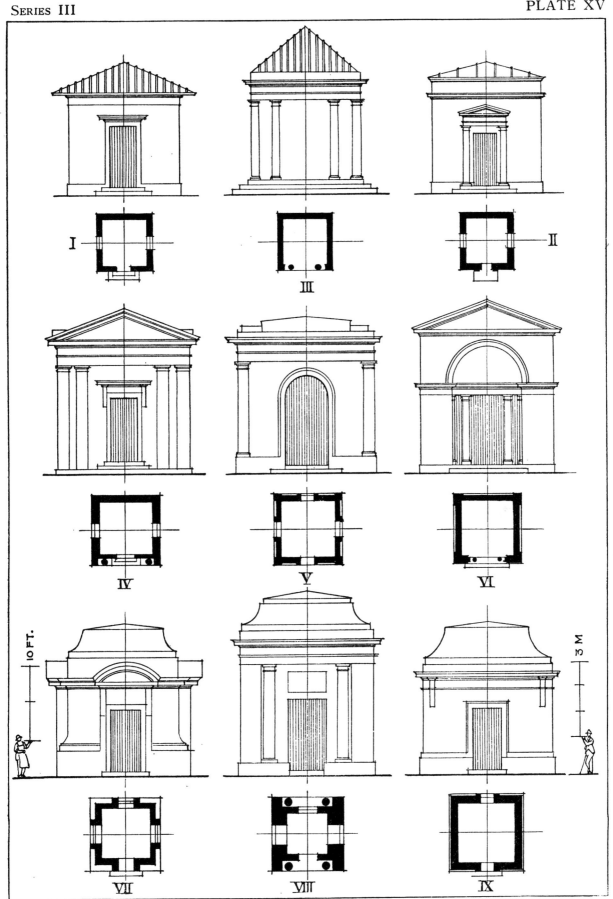

SMALL SQUARE PLANS

I-IX. GENERAL TYPES DRAWN FROM ENGLISH AND FRENCH EXAMPLES

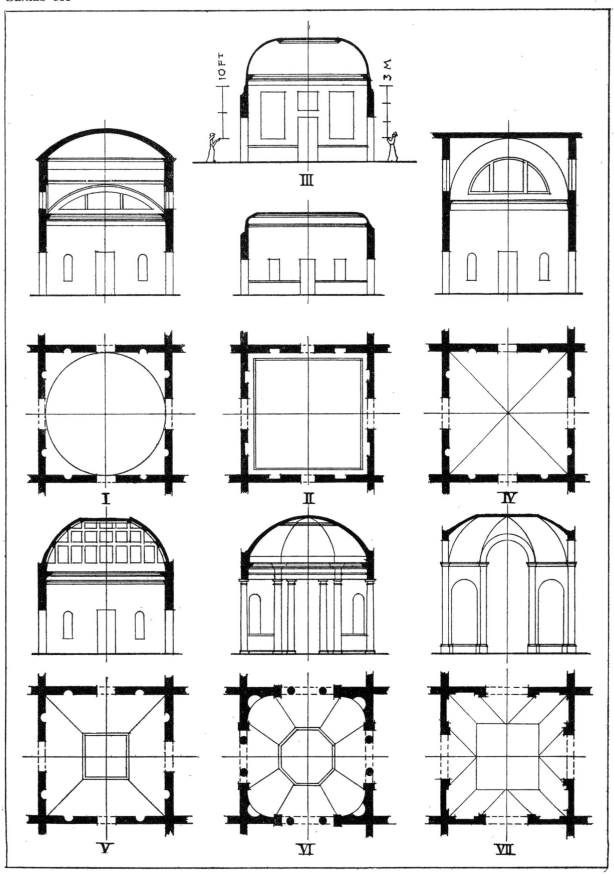

SQUARE PLANS DISPOSED FOR INTERIOR EFFECT

I-VII.   GENERAL TYPES DRAWN FROM ENGLISH, FRENCH AND ITALIAN EXAMPLES.

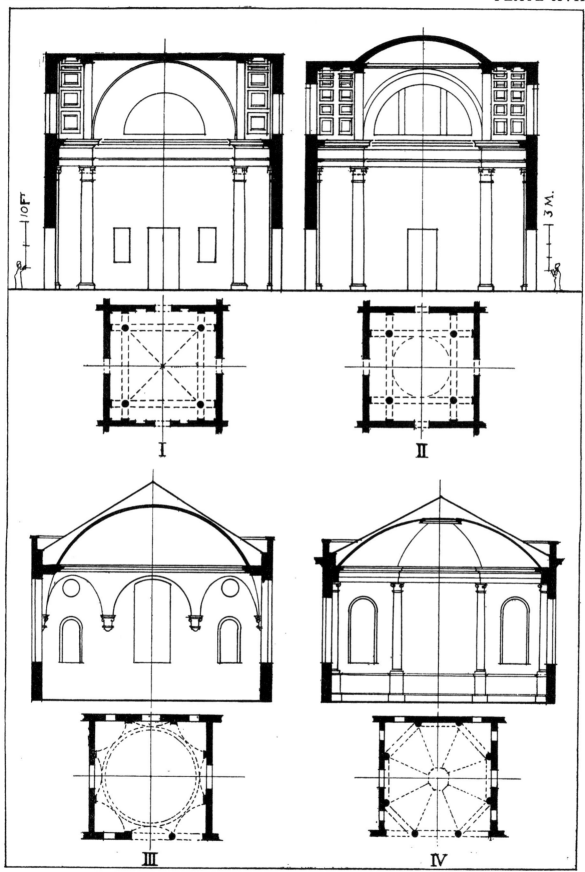

SQUARE HALLS WITH VAULTED AND DOMICAL CEILINGS

I-II.   GENERAL TYPES WITH COFFERED VAULTS.
III   DOMED ON EIGHT "PENDENTIVES," BASED ON CHURCH OF ST. MARY, ABCHURCH, DESIGNED BY SIR CHRISTOPHER WREN.
IV   EIGHT-SIDED DOME, BASED ON CHURCH OF ST. SWITHIN, DESIGNED BY SIR CHRISTOPHER WREN.
(See also Plate XXXVI, Nos. III-VIII, for domical ceilings over rectangular plans designed by Sir Christopher Wren).

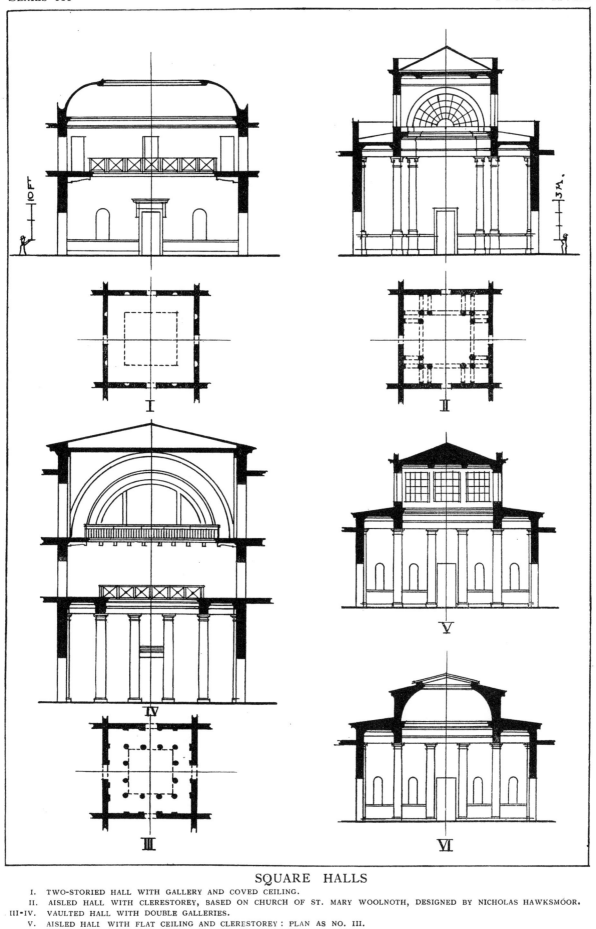

SQUARE HALLS

I.   TWO-STORIED HALL WITH GALLERY AND COVED CEILING.
II.   AISLED HALL WITH CLERESTOREY, BASED ON CHURCH OF ST. MARY WOOLNOTH, DESIGNED BY NICHOLAS HAWKSMÓOR.
III•IV.   VAULTED HALL WITH DOUBLE GALLERIES.
V.   AISLED HALL WITH FLAT CEILING AND CLERESTOREY : PLAN AS NO. III.
VI.   AISLED HALL WITH COVED CEILING AND TOP LIGHTING : PLAN AS NO. III.

IV

THE ROMAN " D " OR TRIBUNE PLAN, SEMI-CIRCULAR AND ELLIPTICAL PLANS.

PLATES XIX TO XXII.

THE plan form of the Greek theatre supplied a motive which was adapted to a variety of purposes during Roman and subsequent periods : this is known as the " D " or Tribune plan, and it has long been accepted as a suitable form for " exedrae " and places of assembly. The earliest examples, such as those supposed to have formed subordinate features of the vast Roman thermae, were covered with semi-domes and were open to the outer air : it was in these places that poets and philosophers declaimed. There are few instances of this type of building to be found intact amongst the ruins of antiquity, but from the conjectural restorations made by various authorities, notably Canina, Durand and Blouet, some examples have been selected for illustration.

The transition from the simple exedra of small size to that of more involved interest is by easy stages, for the principle remains constant and will be readily understood from the examples illustrated. It is possible to vary the system in many ways according to the disposition of columns, colonnades and subsidiary features, while to the plan on a large scale may be added a series of semi-circular niches opening out of the enclosing wall.

The " D " plan as an architectural motive on a large scale first made its appearance at the close of the eighteenth century in the Chambre des Pairs of the Luxembourg, Paris. This was followed by the splendid interior of the Chambre des Députés, which in turn served as a model for the Sorbonne, the most celebrated instance of its use. Further examples of its application can be instanced in the design of the State Capitol, Washington, at the beginning of the last century, and in almost every Parliament House of note on the Continent. In England, however, this ideal form has not received the attention it deserves.

The " D " plan in principle is one intended to give ample space in the auditorium, a central position for the speaker, and scenic display in the architectural treatment. The nearest approach in England to this type of plan is to be seen in the interior design of theatres, particularly those built from about 1770 to 1860, but in nearly every case the theatres built during this period approximate to a horse-shoe rather than to a " D " plan.

It is important that the student should become acquainted with this form of plan as an independent type before attempting to incorporate it in a complicated system of planning in which it is combined with various other features. Generally, such a form becomes the focal point in the arrangement of a building, and its approaches and connections need most careful adjustment. There are occasions when this particular plan can be treated as an isolated building with the addition of a portico, and at other times the basic " D " shape alone can be used as a connecting link, such as a courtyard between groups of buildings. There is no limit to the variety of treatment to which it lends itself, and experience has proved that from many standpoints the " D " plan is satisfactory.

Plate XIX.—This is a perspective view of the interior of the County Hall at Chester designed by Thomas Harrison about 1800. It is interesting as an English example of the treatment of the " D " plan, and shows that the designer was familiar with Roman models as well as with contemporary French practice. The design is chiefly remarkable for the way in which the domical covering is stopped against the flat segmental arch which terminates the " D " form horizontally above the level of the entablature to the peristyle.

Plate XX.—In No. I a simple " D " plan of small size is shown with columnar screen, and two methods of treating the elevation are given ; in No. II the semi-dome is finished against a pediment which is a conspicuous feature of the design, and in No. III the curve of the semi-dome is expressed by a crowning segmental cornice : both are in accordance with Roman precedents. No. IV is an exedra of larger dimensions in which the curve of the dome is revealed to form a frontispiece, and further renderings of the same motive are given in Nos. V to VII. All these examples can be adapted for both internal and external treatments : they can be used for shelters in public parks and features in town furnishing ; as open loggias for the display of sculpture and as incidents in the design of exhibition buildings.

THE SEMI-CIRCULAR OR " HEMICYCLE " PLAN.

Plate XXI.—Another type approaching the " D " in principle is to be found amongst the works of antiquity and of the Renaissance, the system being akin to the more complex form, but resembling the simple exedra without enclosing screen. Nos. I, II and III show a semi-circular plan which can be carried out with a half dome and pediment or segmental parapet, while No. III includes an Order and a pediment, as used by Sir Christopher Wren. Fig. IV is frankly of the arched type with supporting wings and half pediments sympathetic to the half dome, which is coffered. Fig. V is based upon the " Palladian motive." Fig. VI shows a large exedra with pylons on either side against which supporting colonnades terminate : a pleasing variation from the ordinary arrangement of coffering is shown in the semi-dome.

Further examples of this type of plan with concentric peristyles are given on Plates XCIX and C, where they appear as grottoes : see also Fig. 5.

THE ELLIPTICAL PLAN.

Plate XXII.—Except for isolated buildings of large dimensions, this is of rare occurrence in external architecture, the Romans, as far as is known, having confined its application to the amphitheatre. Nevertheless, Serlio, when discussing " divers forms of temples " illustrates an elliptical plan which he describes as next to be preferred to the more perfect circle, and he gives a plan and section for a temple of this form without peristyle and covered by a dome.

The arc of the ellipse changes its direction at different points in the circumference and unless the scale is sufficiently large to enable the eye to grasp and make allowance for the elliptical plan, as in the amphitheatres of the Romans and in great modern buildings, such as the Albert Hall, London, an effect of distortion is produced. The simpler circular plan seems for that reason to possess advantages for external use which have been realised at all periods, perspective inducing effects of elliptical curvature in a circular plan without loss of continuity in the curve of horizontal lines.

Internally the position is different, for the whole form of an apartment can be appreciated at a glance, and the subtle curvature of the ellipse offers great possibilities both on a large and on a small scale. The French architects of the seventeenth and eighteenth centuries, in particular, developed this type of plan in rooms, vestibules and staircases, and their example has been freely followed in England, while not a few notable late Renaissance churches in Italy have elliptical interiors. It is interesting to note, however, that whereas Philibert de l'Orme included great elliptical assembly halls in his plan for the Tuilleries, Paris, Inigo Jones was content to rely upon the circle for the courtyards in his design for the Palace of Whitehall.

Beautiful as are the effects of an elliptical interior, the Pantheon, Rome, and other circular buildings of the largest size show that the simple unbroken horizontal lines within a purely circular building can hardly be improved upon.

On Plate XXII several examples of elliptical plans have been selected to illustrate the theory of the use of this plan form in conjunction with rectangular features in the same way as previously described for the circle and the square (Plate XIV). The advantage of the ellipse for internal use is that it enables a curved apartment to be introduced sympathetic to the lateral axis in positions where it would not be possible to introduce a full circle. Further, it is obvious that where greater length than breadth is desired and the retention of a curved form is a *sine qua non* the ellipse has many advantages. As experimented with by French and Italian architects, the ellipse introduces a new element of fancy which is both ingenious and refreshing.

REFERENCE BOOKS.

Canina, L. *L'Architettura Antica.* 1839-44.

Blouet, G. A. *Restaurations des Thermes Caracalla à Rome.* 1828.

Durand, J. N. L. *Précis des Léçons d'Architecture.* 1802-9.

Joly, J. de. *Palais Bourbon.* (For " D " Plan.)

Wiebeking, C. F. *Architecture Civile.* (For Elliptical Plan.)

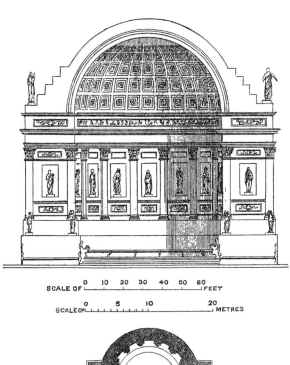

SCALE OF 0 10 20 30 40 50 60 FEET

SCALE OF 0 5 10 20 METRES

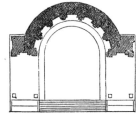

FIG. 5. A ROMAN EXEDRA AS RESTORED BY CANINA.

ROMAN "D" OR TRIBUNE PLAN WITH PERISTYLE

INTERIOR OF THE COUNTY HALL, CHESTER, DESIGNED BY THOMAS HARRISON.

ROMAN "D" OR TRIBUNE PLANS

I-VII.   GENERAL TYPES OF PLAN, ELEVATION AND SECTION.

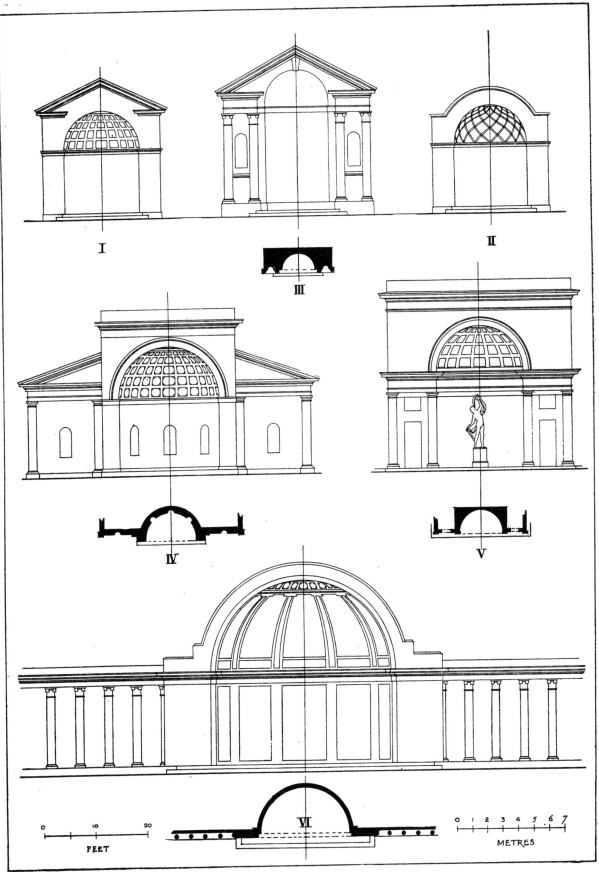

I

II

III

IV

V

VI

0   10   20
FEET

0 1 2 3 4 5 6 7
METRES

SEMI-CIRCULAR OR EXEDRÆ FORMS

I–VI. GENERAL TYPES OF PLAN AND ELEVATION COMBINED WITH SUBSIDIARY FEATURES.

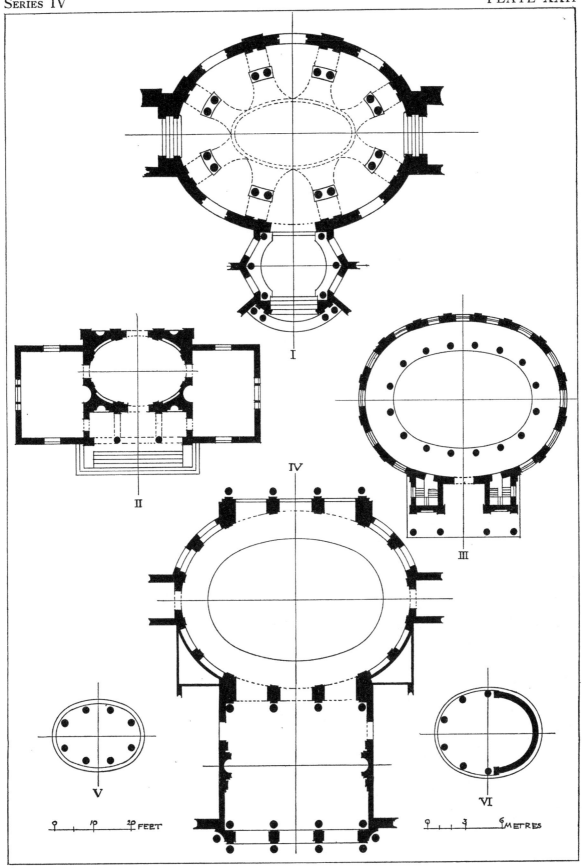

I

II

III

IV

V

VI

0   10   20 FEET

0   1   3   6 METRES

ELLIPTICAL PLANS

I.   BASED ON THE PALAZZO CARIGNANO, TURIN, DESIGNED BY GUARINI.
II. BASED ON AN ORIGINAL STUDY BY JOHN YENN, R.A., IN THE R.I.B.A. LIBRARY.
III. V. GENERAL TYPES.
IV. EXAMPLE : CHATEAU OF VAUX-LE-VICOMTE, DESIGNED BY LOUIS LEVAU.
VI. GENERAL TYPE.

V

OCTAGONAL PLANS.

PLATES XXIII TO XXVI.

THE octagonal plan in architecture conforms to the geometrical principles of the circular: it is introduced for purposes of contrast as well as for picturesque play of line in perspective. For small buildings, such as lodges and guard-rooms, garden temples, shelters for statuary and summer-houses the octagon has many advantages: when used for isolated buildings of large size with a diameter of from 40 to 60 feet, it can be arranged within a colonnade conforming to the inner shape, thereby introducing an interest which prevents a crude appearance. The octagonal plan cannot be successfully employed for isolated buildings with a greater diameter than about 60 feet: should the conditions demand a greater dimension, the figure should be changed into one with many facets, when it approximates closely to the circular or Pantheon type. A very large octagonal building would appear bald in effect in comparison with the reposeful character of a square or circular structure, and it is apparent that the need for interest in the wall surfaces of an octagonal building increases relatively to the size of the structure. The variety of treatment applicable to the octagon is expressed in the outline of the covering: pyramidal roofs and domical coverings preponderate in existing examples, but on a small scale, combinations of concave and convex or " tent " shapes may be introduced with good effect.

The octagonal plan on a large scale is best suited for the treatment of interiors where its extent can be viewed from a central point. In this connection the octagon has been very successfully adapted to rooms with coved and vaulted ceilings which of necessity have to be lit from the top.

Plate XXIII.—The plan of an open octagonal shelter standing in an isolated position is shown in No. I, and alternative treatments of its covering are given in Nos. II and III. Excellent results can be obtained by such simple arrangements of elemental forms. A variety of types suitable for small isolated buildings such as lodges, garden and fishing-houses are shown in the other schemes outlined on this Plate, with coverings ranging from a concealed flat roof to a high eight-sided dome: all these were in constant use by eighteenth and early nineteenth century architects.

Plate XXIV.—The designs shown in Nos. I and II are suitable for the office of a park-keeper or guard-room adjacent to a parade ground, and may be used in duplicate either at the approach to an avenue without a connecting screen or at the junction of two or more roads.   No. III is a simple octagonal building based on a Greek model (Fig. 6), suitable for containing water machinery in connection with a system of fountains and cascades : a stone structure on these lines, however, could be arranged advantageously as a central feature of a pavilion in which the balancing wings could be constructed of lighter material and would be kept comparatively low, allowing the central octagon to dominate.   Nos. IV and V must be considered primarily as ornamental conventions, designed to embellish pleasure-grounds and to form focal points in a scheme of varied interest.   They could be used either for pavilions heading ornamental pools, for shrines enclosing groups of sculpture and for other artificial garden features. All the foregoing types of isolated structure gain considerably from a setting amidst natural scenery, the planting of trees, and the placing of vases and other ornaments adding to their value as decorative features.

Plate XXV.—These two examples give varieties of the larger octagonal building with surrounding colonnades.   Pyramidal and domed roofs are shown and the designs include the treatment of galleries both internal and external with means of access arranged in the thickness of the walls.   As isolated features, buildings on these lines could be used for a variety of purposes, chiefly for retreats on large estates where they might be situated near lakes or within plantations.   Structures of this kind would also be suitable in connection with pleasure buildings at sea-side resorts or inland spas : they follow eighteenth century models and the uses to which they could be put remain to-day much as they were in the past.   The student, however, must not limit his view of the larger sized octagonal feature to isolated structures, for experience will teach him how to combine this type with wings on two or three axes in order to meet specific requirements.   In that case full advantage can be taken of the external galleries which would lead on to terrace roofs, the central octagon being two-storeyed if required.

Plate XXVI.—The advantages of the octagonal plan as a feature of internal design are obvious when its principles are applied to points of interest, either at the meeting of passage ways or for the novel treatment of a single room.   No. I shows the design of a hall or vestibule used as a centre of circulation with a domed ceiling and the light admitted through a lantern at the top.   No. II has a lofty coved ceiling and is lighted from the sides, and No. III is a variant of No. I with a coved ceiling and lantern light.   The system followed in No. IV is similar to that of No. III with the difference that an Order including a full entablature supports the coved ceiling and lantern. In the vestibule shown in No. V, advantage has been taken of the plan form to develop a system of intersecting vaults which finish against the rim of a circular domical skylight. In the octagonal vestibule shown in No. VI the octagon is repeated above a flat ceiling and continued vertically as a crowning lantern. The octagon is seldom used for ordinary apartments, but in the case of writing-rooms and rooms in the external angles of buildings this plan can be introduced with considerable effect.

REFERENCE BOOKS.

D'Espouy, H. *Fragments de l'Architecture Antique.* 1896-1923.

Chambers, Sir W. *A Treatise on the Decorative Part of Civil Architecture.* 1791.

Krafft, J., and Ransonette, N. *Plans, Coupes, Elevations des plus belles Maisons et des Hotels Construits à Paris et dans les Environs.* 1771-1802.

SCALE OF 0 1 2 3 4 5 10 METRES
SCALE OF 0 10 20 30 FEET

FIG. 6. RESTORATION OF THE "TOWER OF THE WINDS," ATHENS.

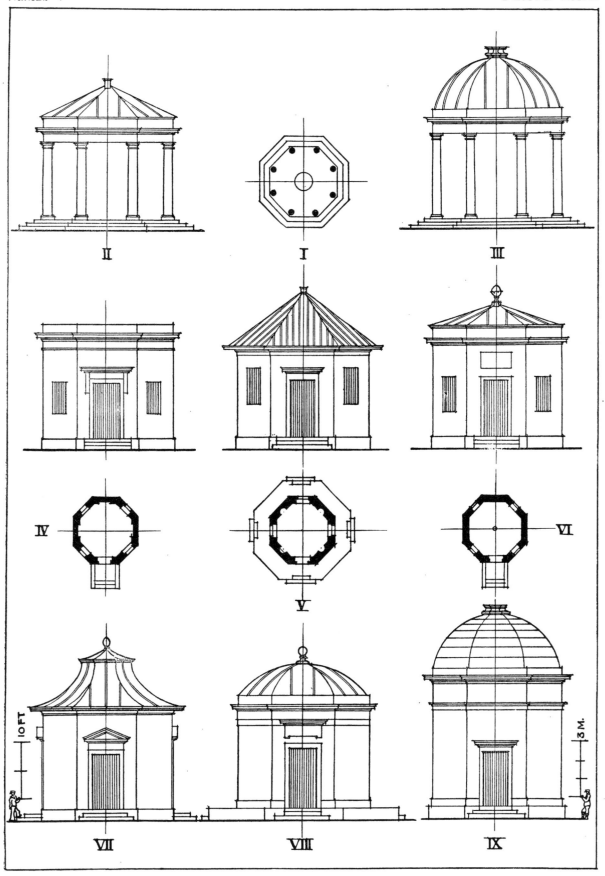

OCTAGONAL PLANS

I-IX.   GENERAL TYPES OF SMALL OCTAGONAL FEATURES, BASED ON ENGLISH AND FRENCH EXAMPLES.

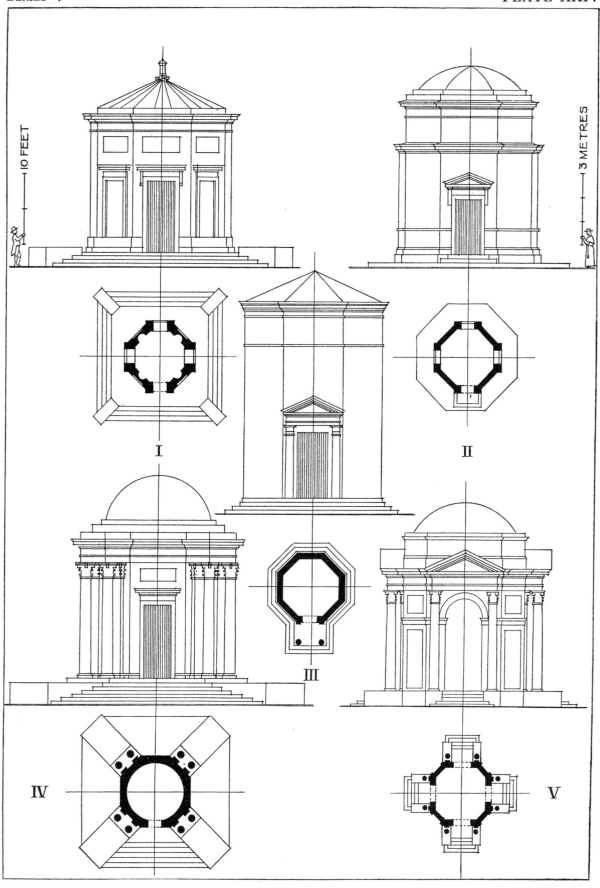

OCTAGONAL PLANS

I-V. GENERAL TYPES. III. EXAMPLE: "TOWER OF THE WINDS," ATHENS.

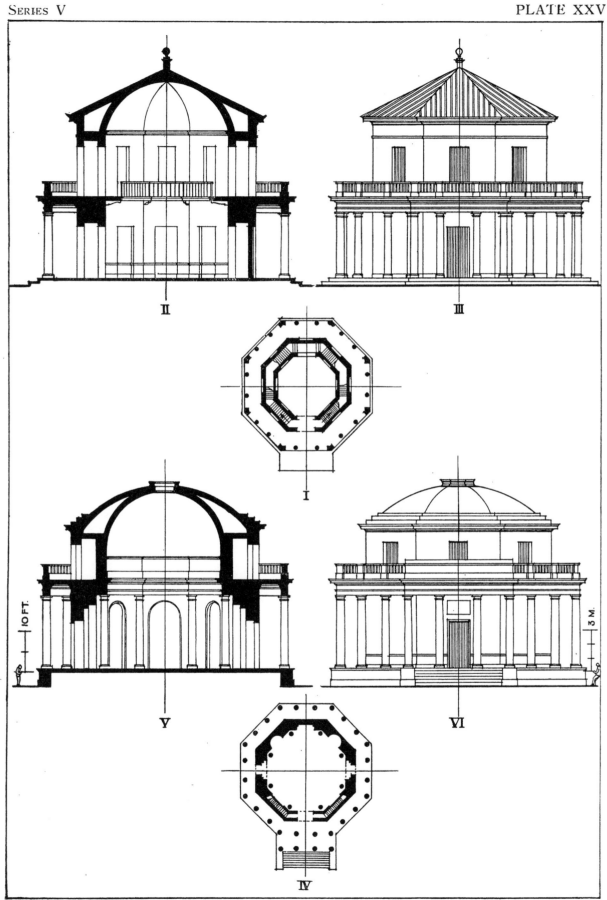

OCTAGONAL PLANS WITH PERISTYLES

I-VI. GENERAL TYPES.

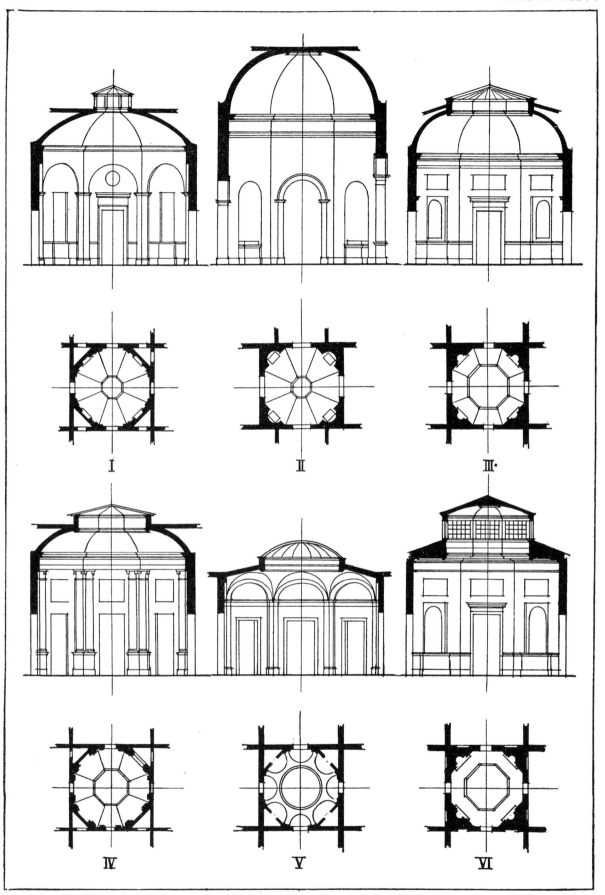

OCTAGONAL PLANS DISPOSED FOR INTERNAL EFFECT

I-VI. GENERAL TYPES.　II. EXAMPLE: HOLKHAM HALL, NORFOLK.　DESIGNED BY WILLIAM KENT.

VI

RECTANGULAR PLANS DISPOSED FOR INTERNAL EFFECT.
PLATES XXVII TO XLV.

A STUDY of the architecture of all periods shows that the rectangle has been widely adopted as a primary form, not only for buildings complete in themselves, but also for the units of complex compositions. In the work of the past no less than in most plans of the present day, this form predominates. This work, however, is intended to treat solely of elementary forms and units, and does not include either the vast plans of the Thermae and Palaces of the Cæsars, or the involved plans of the Renaissance, in all of which the disposition of the rectangle in combination with other primary forms can be studied *ad infinitum*. Throughout domestic building in England and America, especially in houses built in the eighteenth century, variations of the rectangular form are found to be more or less standardised by reason of convenience and tradition. Examples of the exterior treatment of simple rectangular buildings will be found in Series XI.

For interior effect, the rectangular plan is capable of many interpretations. As the parallelogram appears more frequently in the plans of apartments of all kinds than any other figure, the variety of accepted ways of dealing with it is considerable, governed largely by the actual dimensions of the apartment and the method of covering adopted. The rectangular interior like the square, admits of the flat ceiling with or without a cove, as well as numerous applications of the vault, both continuous and intersecting, while scenic effect can be obtained by many dispositions of the dome, either as a central dominating feature with a diameter equal to the shorter side of the rectangular, or over a succession of square compartments within a rectangular plan of large dimensions.

Attention has been given in this Series to the sympathetic proportioning of width, length and height as followed in the best practice. The majority of writers in the past have laid down rules for the proportions of rectangular rooms which are ceiled with flat and coved ceilings, and it is generally agreed that when the length does not exceed twice the breadth the height should be equal to the breadth, and that if a room is coved it should be higher than if it is entirely flat, the cove being equal to one-quarter or one-fifth of the total height of the room. Rectangular rooms when coved may be given a height equal to the breadth plus one-fifth to one-third of the difference between the length and the width, and rooms with vaulted ceilings may have a height to the crown of the vault equal to one-half of the total obtained by adding together the length and the breadth of the room. But rules have rarely been followed so closely as to disregard the dictates of common-sense or to violate conditions imposed by convenience and suitability.

The schemes outlined on the Plates have been taken from many famed buildings which are remarkable for the logical disposition of their plans and sections, and they serve to illustrate the imaginative combinations of straight sided and curved forms which the treatment of the rectangular plan suggests. For all types of buildings for public and civil use they offer valuable suggestions from the standpoint not only of effect but also of utility. Various ways of treating the unbroken rectangle are shown, and where an unencumbered floor space is desired, this form is invariably adopted, but even then many combinations of flat, coved, vaulted and domed coverings are applicable. Relatively to the width, narrow or wide ambulatories can be formed by placing colonnades and piers along two or more sides to enhance the architectural interest of the interior and, by reducing the central span, to facilitate construction and bring about variety of perspective and lighting effects. Colonnades and clerestoreys are found in many of the most impressive interiors that have been raised on the rectangular plan, while halls with colonnades in two storeys with galleries disposed along the sides and at one or both ends, present problems which have been satisfactorily solved in the past. With dimensions that admit of a monumental treatment, the sub-division of the rectangular plan into a series of square compartments on the long axis by means of piers to support domes or intersecting vaults, and by colonnades introduced as sub-motives to support galleries, the rectangular interior assumes its grandest aspect, and apparently complex results may be obtained by the manipulation of elements which in themselves are of extreme simplicity.

Many of the schemes that follow should be studied not only as connecting links in schemes of large dimension, but as being applicable to isolated buildings. These examples of rectangular plan forms cover a wide range of design, and most of the customary arrangements have been considered, but innumerable modifications such as that shown in Fig. 7 will suggest themselves to the student who will realise that finality in composition is neither attainable nor desirable.

Plates XXVII and XXVIII.—These show rectangular rooms with a length equal to twice the breadth. In Plate XXVIII, Nos. I, II and III, the floor space is unbroken by columns or piers. No. I represents the double cube system of proportion in which a flat ceiling, divided into compartments is used with a cove one-fifth the total height of the room : this is suitable for all principal apartments with a width of from twenty to thirty feet.   In No. II a central square is formed by means of arches springing from an attached Order, above which a saucer dome on a low drum is raised : barrel vaults carry on the curve of the transverse

FIG. 7.   INTERIOR OF THE LIBRARY AT MALMAISON.   DESIGNED BY PERCIER AND FONTAINE.

arches, producing a far more elaborate covering than the flat ceiling.   In No. III a continuous segmental ceiling with top-lighting, completes a simpler scheme than the last, but both of these are suitable for halls or waiting places in conjunction with a series of apartments.   Nos. IV, V and VI introduce colonnades, dividing the plan longitudinally into three, the narrow side divisions being carried up a second storey to provide corridors as in No. IV, or ceiled at the level of the top of the colonnade, admitting of a clerestorey, as in No. VI.   The plan given in No. V is common to the three types illustrated, but the various methods of admitting light show to what an extent the architectural disposition can be varied in the section.

The fine room illustrated on Plate XXVII has a segmental ceiling similar in principle to that given in No. III, Plate XXVIII, but without the top light.   It shows a very successful ceiling treatment for a large room with side lighting and is decorative and expressive of the importance of a particular apartment.

Plate XXIX.—In Nos. I-IV is shown a type of simple rectangular plan covered with a barrel vault: the lighting is of the clerestorey type, groined lunettes being arranged at the springing of the vault. This scheme has been used in an isolated building with an apse at one end covered with a semi-dome as shown, but it offers suggestions for the treatment of halls and small places of assembly in which any considerable encroachment on the floor space is undesirable. Nos. V and VI are variations of the foregoing in which additional interest is given to the internal perspective by columns standing clear of the walls and carrying simple intersecting vaults with light admitted through lunettes.

Plate XXX shows further dispositions of the rectangular apartment with clear floor space and interest centred in the coved ceiling. No. I has been selected from Italian practice and is typical of the ceiling treatment common to the halls and apartments of Italian palaces during the sixteenth and seventeenth centuries. No. II is a motive which is found in several of Sir Christopher Wren's churches in the City of London, and by its simplicity recommends itself for the majority of meeting places.

Plate XXXI.—This combines an unbroken rectangular plan with additional lateral features; the ceiling being coved all round gives a rectangular space in the centre above which an elliptical lantern is carried. This excellent scheme is eminently suitable for the entrance hall to a large mansion or to a semi-public building.

Plate XXXII.—This fine rectangular apartment with enriched flat ceiling and side lighting introduces screens at the ends corresponding to the architectural treatment of the side walls. The illustrations show the room as designed by Sir Robert Taylor. The screens in this instance cut off vaulted approaches to the room. Further examples of rectangular rooms with screens across the ends are given on the next two Plates.

Plate XXXIII.—The design of rectangular apartments is often varied by the introduction of semi-circular and segmental ends, while columns supporting nothing more than their entablatures sometimes figure in the form of screens to preserve the original shape of the rectangle. In No. I the vaulted ceiling expresses the plan, and with the columnar screens introduces an imaginative element. In No. II the omission of the columns and the introduction of windows in one of the circular ends produces a useful plan for small reception rooms with flat ceilings. The plan given in No. III follows that of No. I in general idea, the columnar screens being identical, but the ends being segmental are more economical of space. It is, however, none the less effective, and its frequent use with top or side lighting for the dining-rooms of town houses during the eighteenth and early nineteenth centuries proves the esteem in which this type of interior was held.   No. IV shows a rectangular apartment with segmental ends and windows in one side.   The design is simple, the only features being the niches in the thickness of the walls : the motive can be completed with either a flat or a segmental ceiling.   Nos. V and VI combine the leading features of the foregoing and should properly terminate the vista through a suite of rooms.   All these plans offer suggestions for reception-rooms regardless of dimensions.

Plate XXXIV.—This Plate shows internal combinations of square and rectangular compartments.   In Figs. I, II and III, a flat dome is introduced over the centre compartment, and Figs. IV and V show the sub-division of a room of great length in proportion to its width into three compartments, greater importance being given to the central one by the increased height of its ceiling.   Figs. VI and VII show a pleasing sub-division of a large square into subordinate square and rectangular compartments with a dome over the centre.   This motive is one suited to the treatment of a large hall, or it can preferably be used as a unit in a succession of similar groupings.

Plate XXXV.—A rectangular plan for an apartment forming a junction between a group of apartments has of necessity to make provision for lighting from the top.   No. I shows how this can be effected, and it admits of a pleasant architectural interpretation of its purpose in a vertical direction.   No. II shows an effective treatment for a rectangular apartment in which top-lighting becomes auxiliary to partial side lighting.   It is also an original solution of the difficult problem of introducing a domed feature in the centre of a flat ceiling.   Plan No. III shows a variation of the preceding example with an Order introduced as a feature standing clear of the end walls.   Nos. IV and V show a method of lighting a rectangular galleried hall by means of a circular dome carried on pendentives and short lengths of barrel vaulting.   This motive was successfully used in the original booking hall of Euston Station, London, but has been altered beyond recognition.

Plate XXXVI.—Sir Christopher Wren's churches offer rare examples of skill and ingenuity in the handling of rectangular plans both in the introduction of columns and the treatment of ceilings.   Nos. I and II show the interior disposition of St. Stephen's, Walbrook.   Not only is this arrangement suitable for a small church, but its principle can be applied wherever architectural interest combined with effective lighting is desired and where the floor space need be unbroken only in the centre.   In Nos. III, IV and V interest is centred in the upper part of a rectangular apartment, the lighting being obtained through the side and end walls.   A saucer dome carried on pendentives in conjunction with subsidiary barrel vaults completes an effective scheme similar in principle to that given in No. IV on Plate XXXV, but with the omission of the gallery.   The interesting scheme shown in Nos. VI, VII and VIII demonstrates how a simple rectangular plan can assume the character of a complex treatment by the intro-

duction of columns which lead to pleasing contrasts in the ceiling by the use of a saucer dome, inter-secting barrel vaults and flat surfaces.

Plate XXXVII.—This shows an effective arrangement for a gal-leried hall with a flat ceiling in which an Order is introduced as a screen at the level of the gallery. Further dis-positions of galleried halls are given on the succeeding Plates.

Plate XXXVIII.—In places where public business is carried on, it is considered desirable to provide at least one important chamber in which internal effect is

FIG. 8.   INTERIOR SHOWING DOMED COMPARTMENTS AND COLUMNAR SCREENS.
DESIGNED BY C. F. SCHINKEL.

studied as well as the needs of the public and staff.   Adequate lighting should be a primary consideration, and the example shown in Nos. I and II provides a motive suitable for any ordinary contingency.   Two storeys are included with open corridors, which can be adapted to the convenience of any particular office.   In No. III a more usual section applicable to the same plan is given.   No. IV shows an alternative rendering with barrel vaulted ceilings springing from one level, and top lighting over the central area.   In Nos. V and VI the principal difference in the scheme consists in the elimination of the end gallery in favour of an apsidal termination and the introduction of clerestorey lighting.   Nos. VII and VIII show a further development of the plan formation with a variation in the arrangement of the vaulting and the omission of all galleries.   Such schemes can be used for a variety of buildings such as small exchanges, or auction and assembly rooms, and they can be adapted to become important features, such as waiting spaces in large public buildings.

Plate XXXIX.—The provision of a gallery on one side only is occasionally called for in the planning of council chambers, large halls in country houses and rooms lighted from one side. Fig. I shows an effective arrangement of columns screening a gallery and subsidiary corridor below : this arrangement has to some extent been happily followed by Sir Christopher Wren in the design of some of the City churches. In Fig. II a rectangular plan is shown with the addition of a gallery at one end, an arrangement which lends itself to fine internal effect. A feature is made of the clerestorey which is formed in a groined cove supporting the flat ceiling. Special emphasis is given to the junction of the gallery with the side walls by the manipulation of the end bay.

Plate XL.—The possibilities of the rectangular hall with colonnades and coved ceiling have been realised in more than one princely mansion in which it has been desired that scenic effect should impress the spectator immediately upon entering. In No. I a fine scheme is shown with steps at the head of the plan leading to the ambulatories raised high above the main floor level and giving access to the principal reception rooms. The beauty of the plan is expressed in the apsidal treatment and the manner in which the curved lines of the colonnade complete the vista. The Order is introduced on a large scale in No. II, but the hall is in simpler relation to the circular domed apartment on the same level. The ambulatories admit of communication being made with subsidiary chambers at any point on either side of the hall, thereby ensuring easy circulation independently of the central floor space.

Plate XLI and XLII.—The problem of a gallery forming part of the construction of a hall of large dimensions is one constantly facing the designer. The galleried hall illustrated on Plate XLI is eminently suitable to an interior scheme calling for rich interest and perspective effects. The introduction of columnar screens avoids abrupt junctions between the hall and the apartments at each end, which are ceiled at a lower level.

The example given in No. I, Plate XLII, shows a very successful interpretation which not only allows the main floor space to be unencumbered, but admits of recesses and small rooms being grouped geometrically around it. Access to the gallery is provided : this type of plan is especially suited to libraries and reading rooms where seclusion and easy access to books is desirable. In No. II is shown one of those rare examples in which the superimposition of two attached Orders gives the key to the architectural treatment. A gallery carried on brackets is introduced all round and notice should be taken of the treatment of the ceiling and the spacing of the Order on the end walls. Such a design lends itself to the purposes of banqueting halls and museums.

Plate XLIII.—On this and the last Plates of this Series are shown rectangular halls of large size which are sub-divided longitudinally by piers and colonnades. In No. I the plan provides narrow ambulatories on both sides; the main piers carry arches and barrel vaults which enclose a series of square compartments above which saucer domes are raised. Colonnades introduced between the piers carry galleries, in the case of a detached building such as a museum or pavilion, but when used as a connecting link in a large composition, means of communication at a higher level would be afforded over the colonnade, light being admitted in either case through large lunettes on the clerestorey principle. An idea of the perspective effect of this type of interior can be obtained from Fig. 8. Nos. IV-VI give a further development of the foregoing: the principle of the sub-division of the plan, providing a series of central square compartments covered with intersecting vaults or saucer domes being identical.

FIG. 9. GREAT HALL IN THE PALACE OF THE TUILERIES, PARIS, SHOWING DOMED COMPARTMENTS AND COLUMNAR SUPPORTS, DESIGNED BY PERCIER AND FONTAINE.

The introduction of colonnades as sub-motives between the piers and the provision of galleries or means of communication are also similar. This fine design is shown as a complete scheme for a detached building with external peristyle.

Plate XLIV.—Wherever classic models have been followed, the system evolved by the Romans for the central halls of the great Thermae has been employed by architects dealing with the problem of vast places of assembly.   The two schemes shown on this Plate are based directly on Roman precedent.   No. I is similar in principle to Nos. IV-VI on the previous Plate, but instead of colonnades supporting galleries between the piers, the dimensions here are so great that the main supporting wall is in line with the piers so that the upper part of the hall does not extend in width beyond them, the outer walls enclosing a series of apartments at a lower level, and the colonnades becoming columnar screens. The central area is effectively covered by saucer domes over the three square compartments somewhat similar to the arrangement shown in Fig. 9.

No. II shows a development in which piers without colonnades or screens are the chief interest.   These two designs are capable of more variations than can be indicated here : they have been chosen as representative of the long series of buildings of this type which have come into existence in modern times.

Plate XLV.—These two rectangular motives of large dimension are monumental in conception.   No. I shows a scheme for a large unbroken central area for general use, combined with subsidiary apartments at three levels under the same roof.   It is capable of translation into terms of almost any public or state building, and the majority of bourses and customs houses have been designed on these lines.   The internal arrangement of walls and vaulting with the provision for lighting shown could be used in connection with almost any dominant feature in a large composition that is likely to arise in practice.   No. II should be studied for its fine architectural character and for the logical disposition of its parts both horizontally and vertically, culminating in the great barrel vault.   In this will be found a composition primarily suitable for halls on a grand scale with gallery accommodation and circulating corridors.   The lighting is adequate and the galleries are an integral part of the scheme and contribute to its effect.   With one or more external colonnades, the treatment admits of dominant expression being given externally to the central portion of the hall.

REFERENCE BOOKS.

Adam, Robert and James. *The Works in Architecture of,* 1778.

Clayton, J. *Works of Sir Christopher Wren.* 1848-9.

Klenze, Leo von. *Anweisung zur Architectur des Christlichen Culturs.* 1834.

Lowell, Guy. *Smaller Italian Villas and Farmhouses.* 1922.

London Interiors. 1841-44.

Percier, C., et Fontaine, P. *Choix de plus Cèlebrès Maisons de Plaisance de Rome et ses Environs,* 1824.

Pyne, H. *History of the Royal Residences.* 1819.

Richardson, A. E. *Monumental Classic Architecture in Great Britain and Ireland in the Eighteenth and Nineteenth Centuries.* 1914.

Schinkel, C. F. *Sammlung Architectonischer Entwürfe.* 1836.

PLATE XXVII

RECTANGULAR INTERIOR WITH SEGMENTAL COFFERED CEILING

ASSEMBLY ROOM AT THE EXCHANGE, BELFAST, DESIGNED BY SIR ROBERT TAYLOR.

PLATE XXVIII

RECTANGULAR PLANS DISPOSED FOR INTERNAL EFFECT

I–VI. GENERAL TYPES WITH COVED, VAULTED AND DOMED CEILINGS.

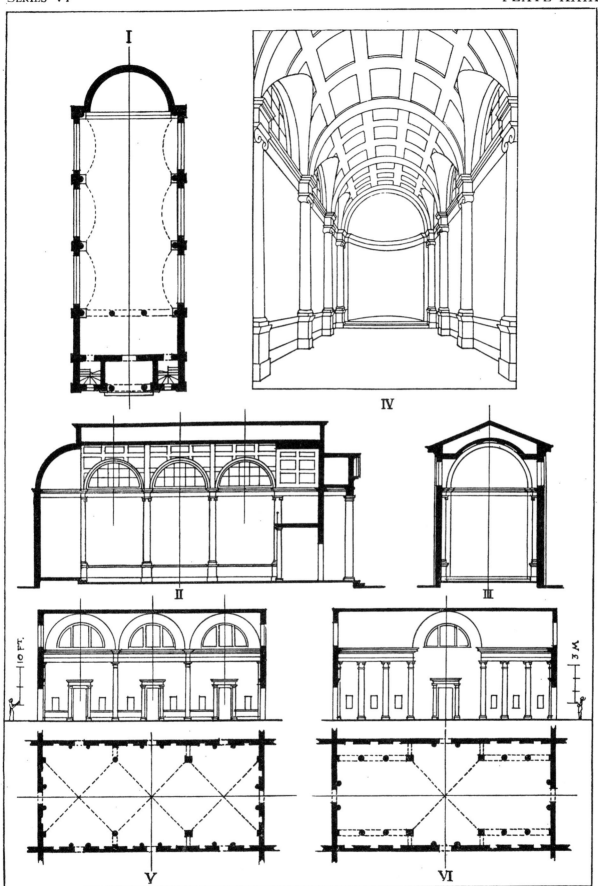

I

IV

II

III

10 FT.

3 FT.

V

VI

RECTANGULAR HALLS WITH VAULTED CEILINGS

I-IV. BASED ON THE CHURCH OF ALL HALLOWS, LONDON WALL, DESIGNED BY GEORGE DANCE THE YOUNGER.
V-VI. GENERAL TYPES.

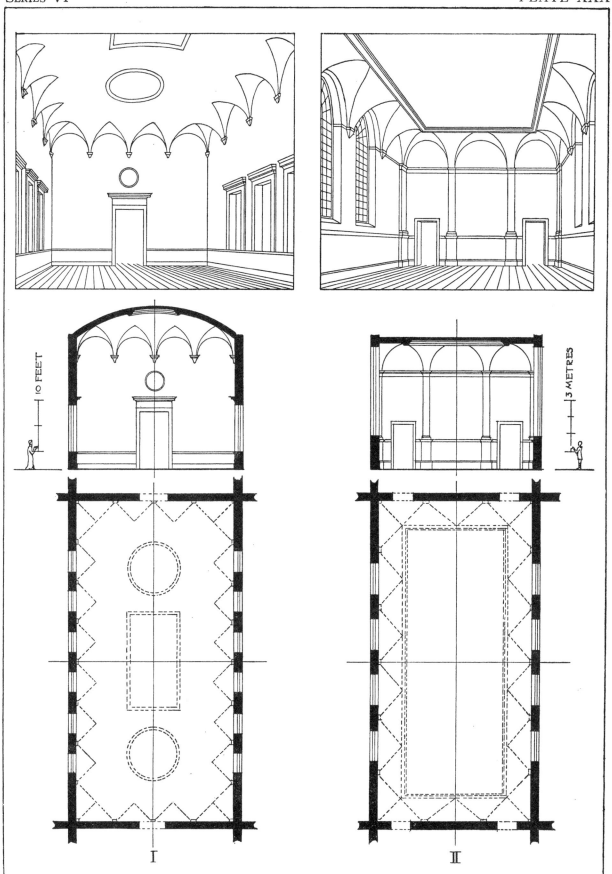

10 FEET

3 METRES

I

II

RECTANGULAR HALLS WITH COVED CEILINGS

I.   BASED ON ITALIAN PRACTICE, SIXTEENTH AND SEVENTEENTH CENTURIES.
II. BASED ON ENGLISH PRACTICE, SEVENTEENTH AND EIGHTEENTH CENTURIES.

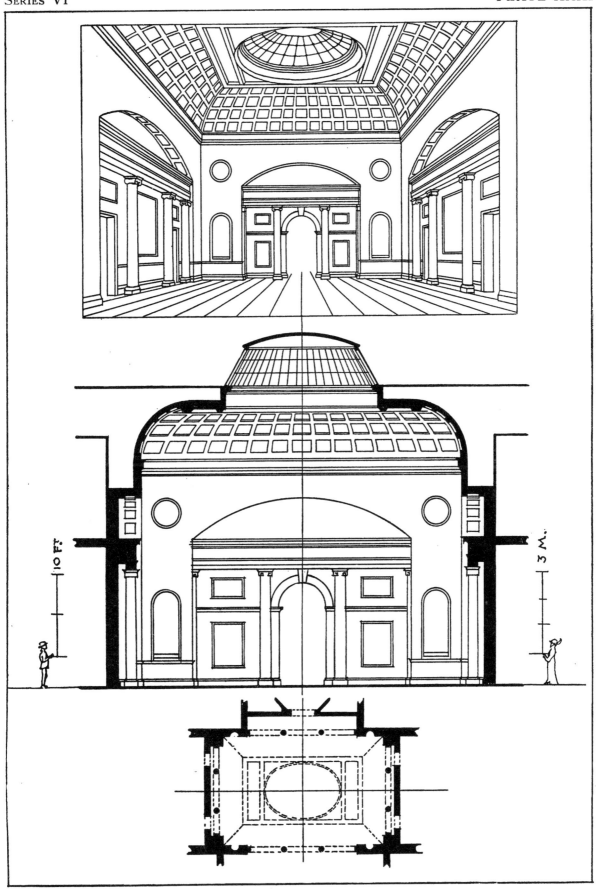

RECTANGULAR HALL WITH COVED CEILING AND LANTERN LIGHT

EXAMPLE : CARLTON HOUSE, LONDON (NO LONGER EXISTING), DESIGNED BY HENRY HOLLAND.

RECTANGULAR INTERIOR WITH COLUMNAR SCREENS AND SIDE LIGHTING

THE COURT ROOM, BANK OF ENGLAND, LONDON, DESIGNED BY SIR ROBERT TAYLOR.

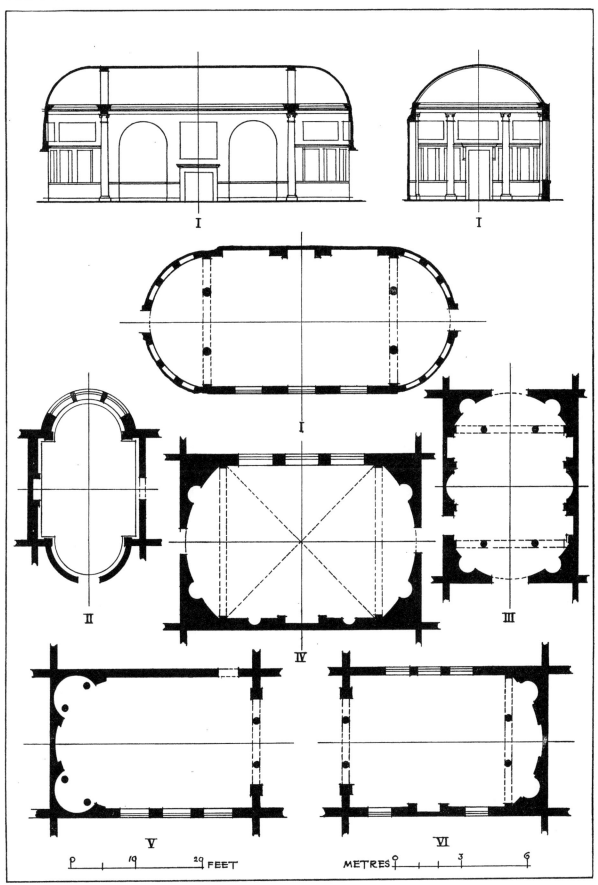

RECTANGULAR APARTMENTS WITH CURVED ENDS AND SCREENS

I. EXAMPLE: THE LIBRARY, KENWOOD, DESIGNED BY THE BROTHERS ADAM.
II-VI. GENERAL TYPES BASED ON EIGHTEENTH CENTURY PRACTICE IN ENGLAND.

PLATE XXXIV

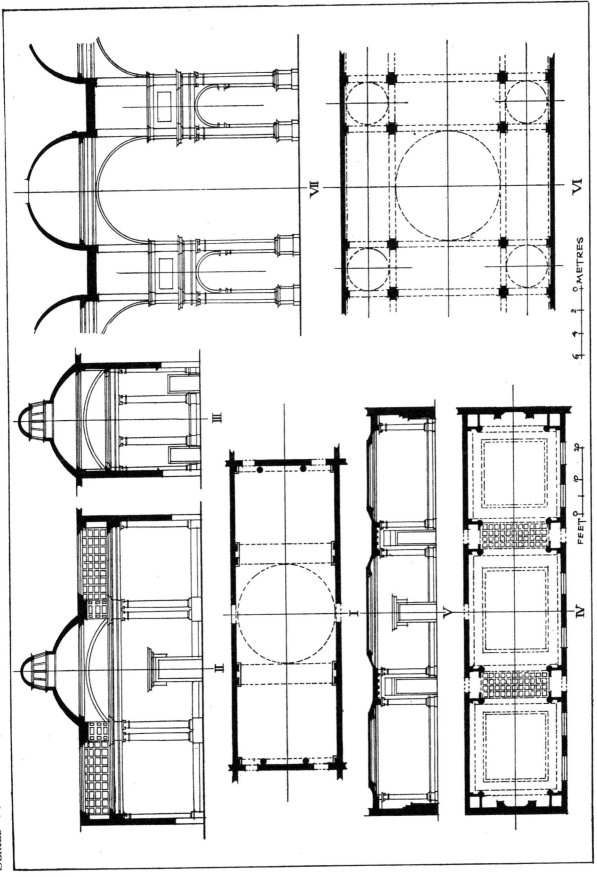

RECTANGULAR AND SQUARE COMPARTMENTS COMBINED FOR INTERNAL EFFECT

I-III. EXAMPLE: OLD CUTLER'S HALL, SHEFFIELD, DESIGNED BY SAMUEL WORTH.
IV-V. EXAMPLE: THE REFORM CLUB, LONDON, DESIGNED BY SIR CHARLES BARRY.
VI-VII. EXAMPLE: CHURCH OF S. SALVATORE, VENICE, DESIGNED BY T. LOMBARDO.

PLATE XXXV

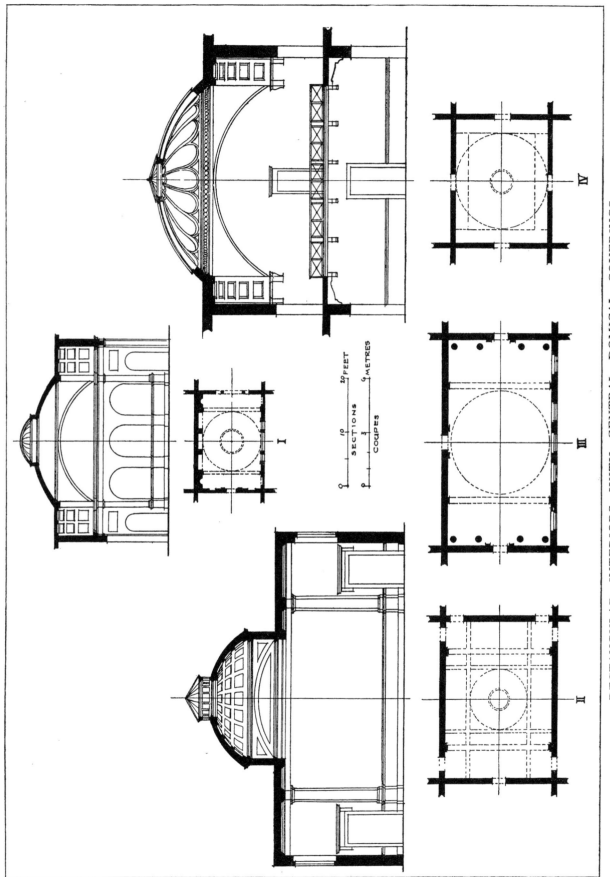

RECTANGULAR INTERIORS WITH CENTRAL DOMICAL COVERINGS

I.   EXAMPLE : OLD DERBY HOUSE, DESIGNED BY THE BROTHERS ADAM.
II. EXAMPLE : THE LIBRARY, ROYAL INSTITUTE OF BRITISH ARCHITECTS, LONDON, DESIGNED BY JAMES WYATT.
III. GENERAL TYPE. (COMPARE WITH NOS. I-III, PLATE XXXIV.
IV. GALLERIED HALL, BASED ON OLD BOOKING HALL, EUSTON STATION, LONDON, DESIGNED BY P. HARDWICK (SINCE REMODELLED).

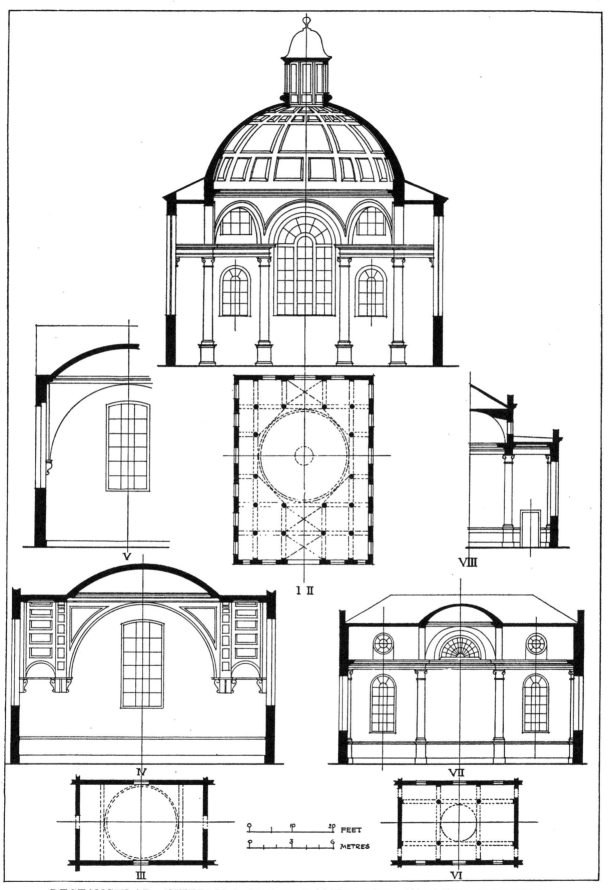

RECTANGULAR INTERIORS WITH DOMED AND VAULTED CEILINGS

BASED ON EXAMPLES IN THE CHURCHES IN THE CITY OF LONDON, DESIGNED BY SIR CHRISTOPHER WREN.
I-II. ST. STEPHEN, WALBROOK. III-V. ST. MILDRED, BREAD STREET. VI-VIII. ST. MARY-AT-HILL.
SEE ALSO PLATE XVII, NOS. III AND IV, FOR DOMICAL CEILINGS OVER SQUARE PLANS, ALSO DESIGNED BY SIR CHRISTOPHER WREN.

RECTANGULAR HALL WITH GALLERIES

CONCERT HALL IN THE IMPERIAL THEATRE, BERLIN, DESIGNED BY C. F. SCHINKEL.

PLATE XXXVIII

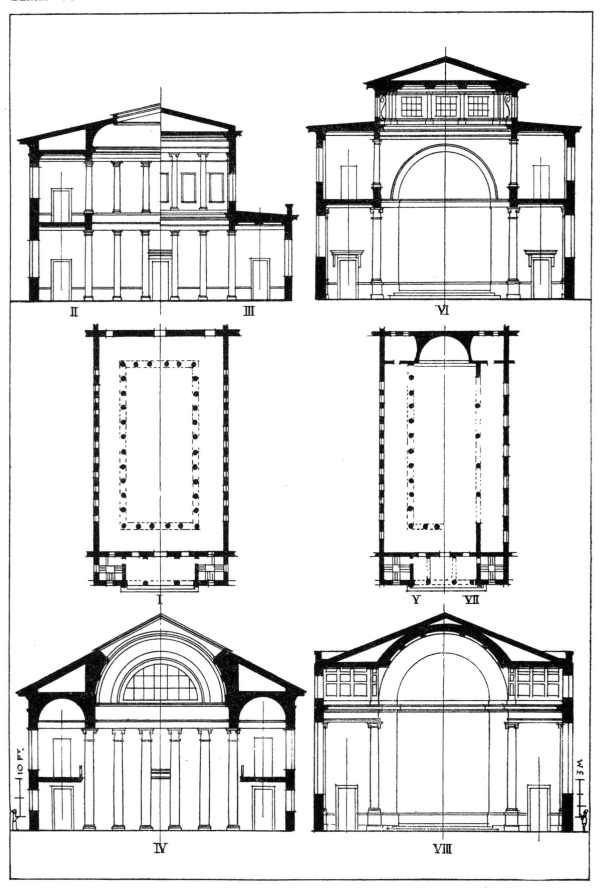

RECTANGULAR HALLS WITH COLONNADES

I-VIII.   GENERAL TYPES SHOWING VARIETIES OF ROOFING AND LIGHTING.

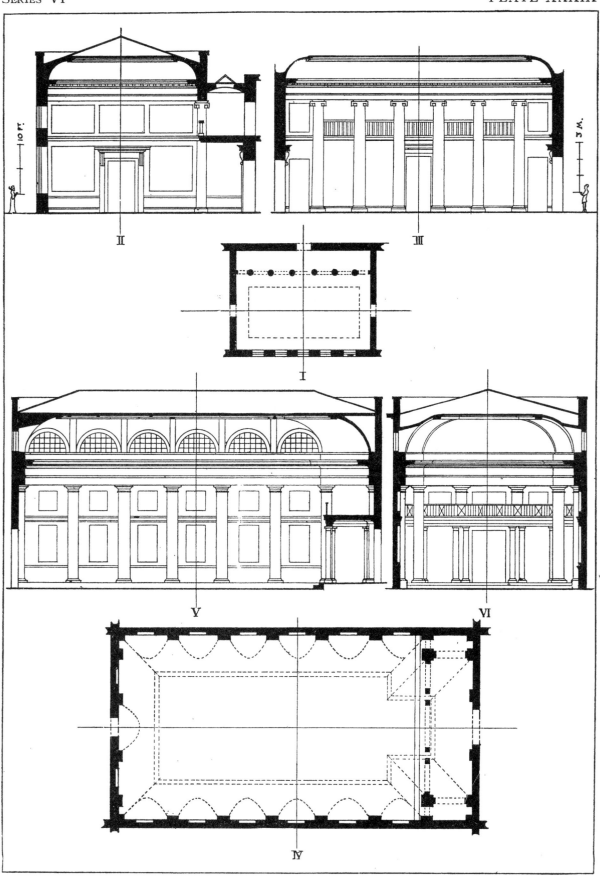

RECTANGULAR HALLS WITH GALLERY ON ONE SIDE ONLY

I-III. GENERAL TYPE.
IV-VI. EXAMPLE: FREEMASON'S HALL, LONDON, DESIGNED BY THOMAS SANDBY.

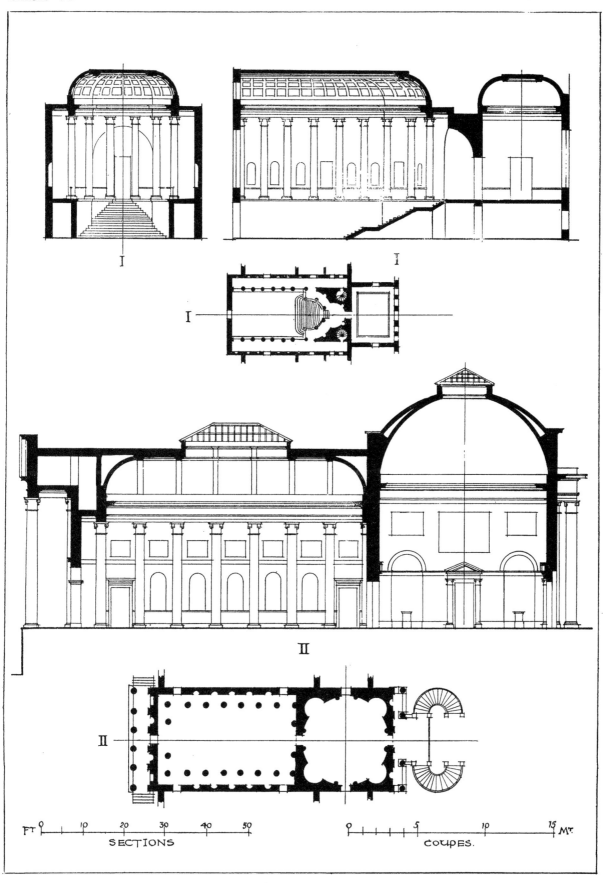

RECTANGULAR ENTRANCE HALLS WITH COLONNADES AND COVED CEILINGS

I. BASED ON HOLKHAM HALL, NORFOLK, DESIGNED BY WILLIAM KENT.
II. BASED ON KEDLESTON HALL, DERBYSHIRE, DESIGNED BY JAMES PAINE.

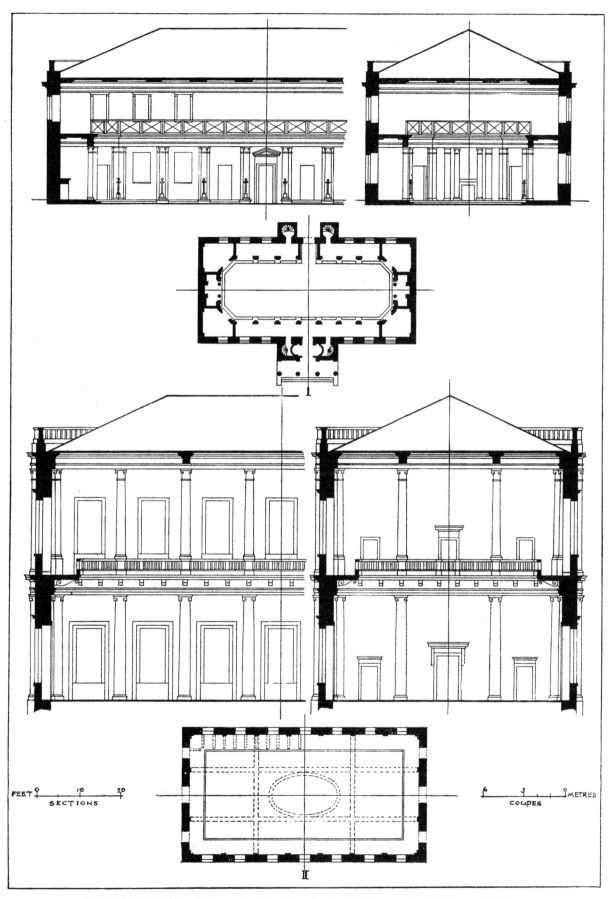

FEET 0   10   20   SECTIONS   6   METRES   COUPES

RECTANGULAR HALLS WITH GALLERIES ON FOUR SIDES

I. EXAMPLE: LIBRARY OF THE LONDON INSTITUTION, DESIGNED BY WILLIAM BROOKS.
II. EXAMPLE: THE BANQUETING HALL, WHITEHALL, DESIGNED BY INIGO JONES.

PLATE XLI

INTERIOR OF RECTANGULAR GALLERIED HALL

HEVENINGHAM HALL, SUFFOLK, DESIGNED BY SIR ROBERT TAYLOR.

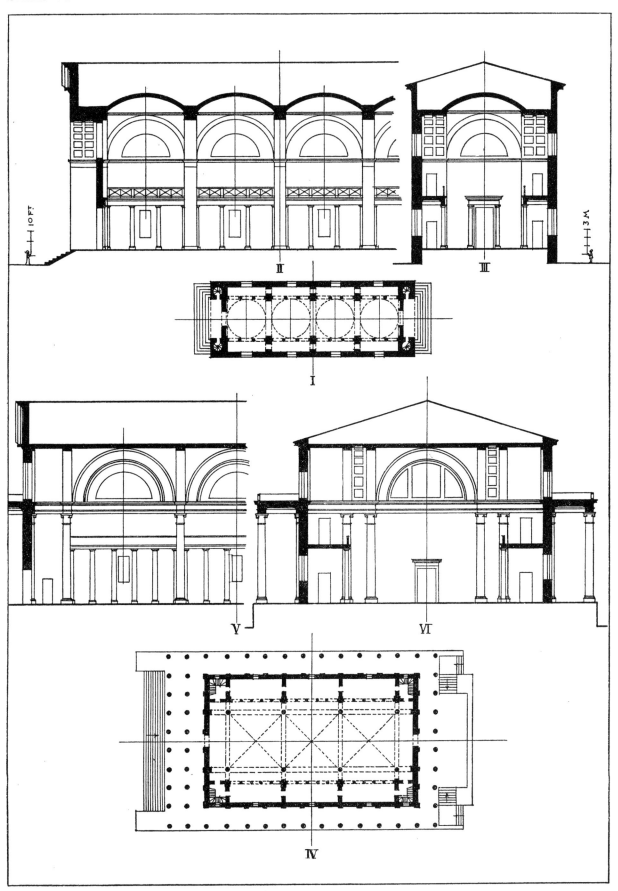

LARGE RECTANGULAR HALLS WITH PIERS AND COLONNADES

I.   GENERAL TYPE WITH CENTRAL SQUARE COMPARTMENTS DOMED.

II. GENERAL TYPE WITH CENTRAL SQUARE COMPARTMENTS CROSS VAULTED.

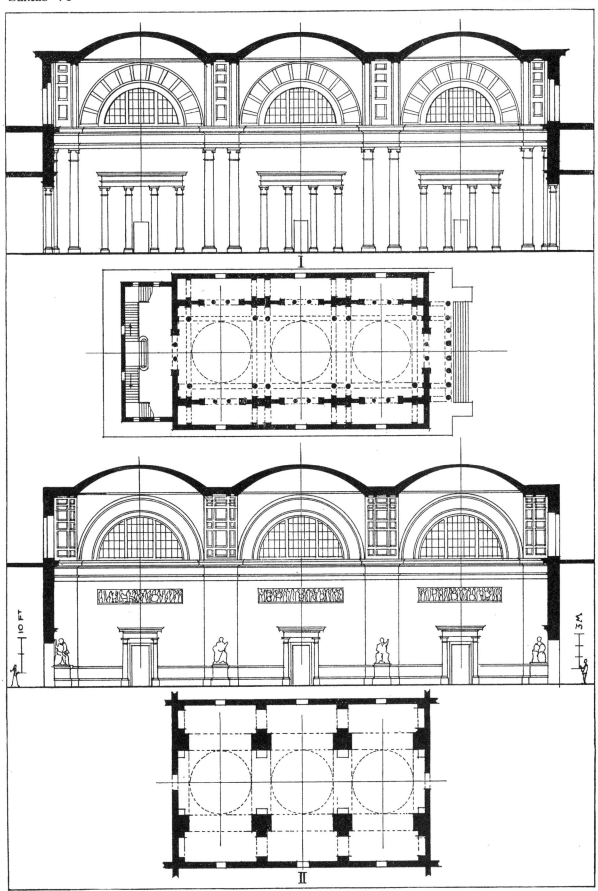

I

10 FT

3 M

II

LARGE RECTANGULAR HALLS WITH PIERS AND COLONNADES

I–II.   BASED ON ROMAN PRACTICE WITH CENTRAL SQUARE COMPARTMENTS DOMED.

PLATE XLV

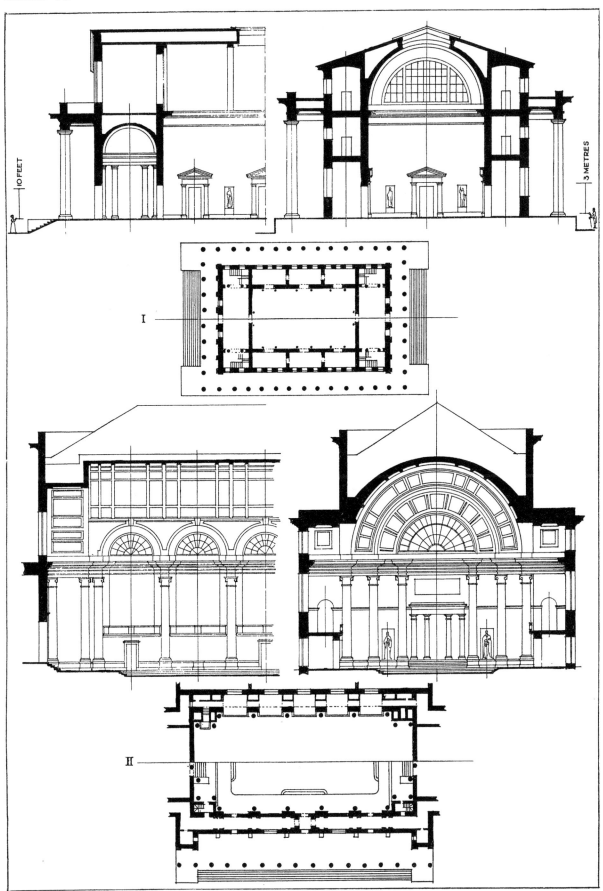

10 FEET

3 METRES

I

II

LARGE RECTANGULAR HALLS WITH BARREL VAULTS

I. EXAMPLE: THE BOURSE, PETROGRAD, DESIGNED BY THOMAS DE THOMON.

II EXAMPLE. ST. GEORGE'S HALL, LIVERPOOL, DESIGNED BY JAMES ELMES.

VII

INTERNAL CORRIDORS.

PLATES XLVI AND XLVII.

THE disposition of corridors in a plan is determined by the needs of circulation in connection with specific apartments, halls, vestibules and staircases, while it is also governed by the uses of the building. For the purposes of this work, ordinary passage-ways are dealt with, such as allow of various methods of architectural treatment. No hard and fast rules can be laid down as to the proportion of length to width in a corridor, but it is safe to assume that the height should not exceed one and a half times the width : that it should be neither too tall nor excessively low, and that unlike the " long gallery " its use is to expedite circulation and not to encourage halting places. Corridors play an important part in the internal perspective of buildings, and should be designed to link up larger features and to give direct communication to salient points. They should not be thought of as bare passages, but should be divided in their length into bays of suitable width, and treated in a variety of ways to check the impression of undue length and to assist the mind of the spectator to realise that a general scale runs through the building. The corridor is important, and it should bear sympathetic relation to the design and proportion of adjacent halls and apartments.

In a long corridor, it is usual to divide the length into a number of bays corresponding to the width, and if possible these divisions should accord with the general proportions of the plan in order to preserve rhythm. Corridors designed on these lines can be covered with flat, semi-circular or segmental ceilings or with intersecting vaults springing from pilasters or corbels, while numerous arrangements of saucer domes with or without pendentives are equally permissible.

Sometimes a coupled pilaster Order can be introduced with good effect, but this should be reserved for important corridors and be designed in connection with axial points, such as the entrances to apartments opening directly off the corridor on either side. Every care must be given both in plan and elevation to the adjustment of a corridor to a feature of greater importance in the internal arrangement of a building : there should be no crude junctions. Generally speaking, corridors must not be too long and, if possible, should be widened at the centre by means of a top-lighted vestibule or by a staircase hall intersecting one side without breaking the flow of traffic. Reference to the staircase Plates, Nos. LVI and LXII, will convey an idea of this arrangement. Corridors can be lighted from the ends, sides, or points at the top where skylights can be conveniently inserted : where such lighting is debarred, however, the staircase and the hall should be so arranged as to light the corridor throughout its length.

The corridor and passage-way became a feature of English domestic architecture during the second half of the eighteenth century when considerable changes from the earlier types were introduced into the planning of the town house, and the corridor with flat or vaulted ceiling came into general use.   It was further developed by the Brothers Adam and reached its zenith in this country under the guidance of Sir John Soane.   During the Victorian period, taste reverted to pure Italian models taken from the courtyards of Renaissance palaces, and examples on a large scale are to be seen at the Foreign Office in Whitehall.   The student, however, is advised to give his attention particularly to the work of the late eighteenth century architects in order to understand the more graceful and rational treatments of the subject.

A great variety of types can be evolved in this particular branch of design : such embellishments as niches for statuary, coupled pilasters, complete Orders, arcades and other features can be reserved for application to corridors where display is requisite, but no purpose would be served by illustrating types embodying these attributes, which can only be applied when a full knowledge of the problem in hand has been acquired.

Plate XLVI.—In Nos. I to IX, inclusive, are shown various arrangements for the treatment of simple corridors, to all of which the plans Nos. III and VI apply.   All these show the corridor divided into bays by means of flat pilasters, which may be coupled if occasion requires, as in No. VII.   The coverings include flat ceilings with cross beams, barrel vaults, segmental and elliptical ceilings with coffering arranged in a variety of ways.   The wall surfaces may be treated with a dado having capping and base and large panels above it, or they may be left plain, the base and capping of the pilasters being continued the length of the corridor.   In Nos. X to XV, inclusive, are shown methods of using intersecting vaults over corridors, and the plan No. X applies equally whether the vaults are semi-circular or elliptical.   In Nos. XIII and XV the vault springs from corbels or brackets, and a series of lunettes are formed above the impost.   Intersecting vaults carried on corbels with well designed lunettes figured frequently in late eighteenth and early nineteenth century practice.

Plate XLVII.—This introduces several designs of richer type in which the compartments are square and are covered with saucer domes on pendentives. The plan No. I applies to these arrangements whether the pendentives are carried on semi-circular, segmental or elliptical arches.   A corridor three bays in length is shown in Nos. V and VI in which interest is given by a combination of intersecting vaults on either side of a central compartment which is covered with a saucer dome.   Various combinations are permissible on the lines indicated.

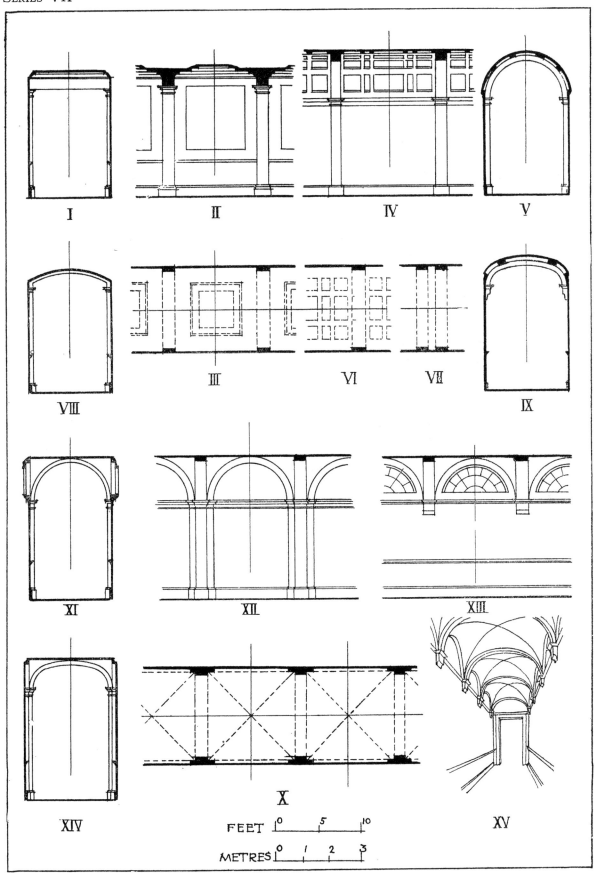

INTERNAL CORRIDORS

I-XV. GENERAL TYPES WITH FLAT AND VAULTED CEILINGS.

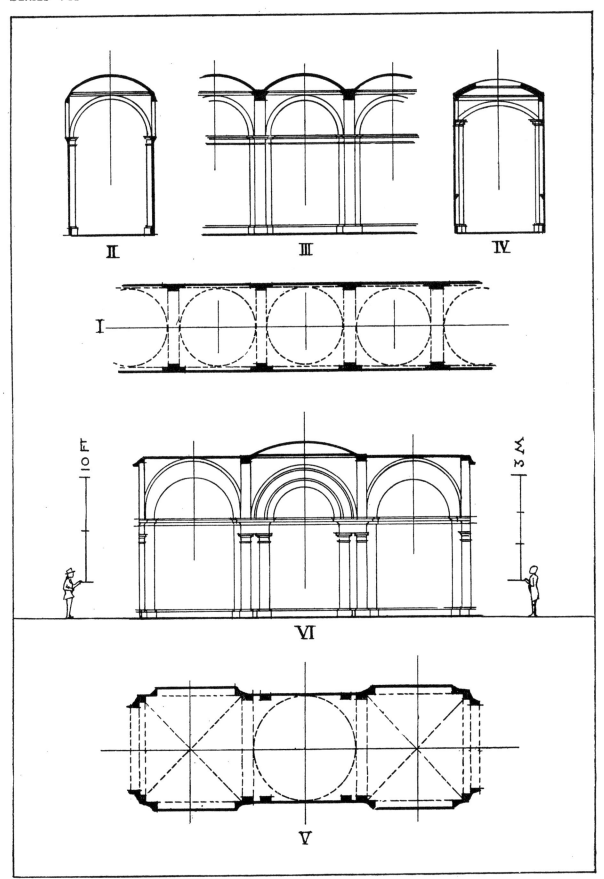

INTERNAL CORRIDORS

I-IV.   GENERAL TYPES WITH SQUARE DOMED COMPARTMENTS.
V-VI.   EXAMPLE : ELY HOUSE, DOVER STREET, LONDON, DESIGNED BY SIR ROBERT TAYLOR.

VIII

VESTIBULES, VAULTED LOGGIAS AND COVERED APPROACHES.

PLATES XLVIII TO LIII.

THE functions of the vestibule are many; and according to its main purpose, it may be considered to fall into two distinct types: first, when it serves as an ante-room to a large waiting hall or other apartment (Fig. 10), and secondly, when it is used to give access to a building or courtyard from the street and is designed to accommodate both foot and wheeled traffic. The theory underlying the design of the latter form of vestibule is similar to that governing the design of the corridor and many of the features described in Series VII apply to this type, which is primarily a means of communication. In features of this kind it is usual to adopt a scheme of vaulting in order to give an imposing effect, and one of two systems is generally followed. Either a series of intersecting vaults is carried on supports to form a three-way disposition conforming to the main axis, in which case the passages are equally disposed—slightly greater width being given to the central one—or the treatment follows the well-known "Palladian motive" in which the central thoroughfare is much wider and is spanned by a barrel vault, while the side ways are covered with flat ceilings at the level of the cornice from which the central vault springs. There are few examples of either of these arrangements to be found in England where planning has not been developed on the principle of the internal courtyard, and with the exception of the magnificent vestibule designed by Sir William Chambers to connect the Strand front of Somerset House with the courtyard (Plate XLIX), there is nothing approaching the grand character of the vestibules often found in palaces of Italian cities. The vestibule in France has been developed according to Italian precedent for close upon three centuries, and it is to be seen in its modern form in the public and private buildings of Paris where unique conditions of planning have favoured its evolution on those lines. Some attempt has been made in this country, not without success, to incorporate the vestibule in modern public buildings, such as the entrances to the India and Foreign Offices as well as certain new Government buildings in Whitehall.

The problem of a vestibule designed for wheeled traffic with two distinct thoroughfares, in addition to passage-ways for pedestrians, is likely to confront the architect, and this demands especial consideration in order to overcome certain difficulties which arise from æsthetic causes, because such an arrangement is never good unless the idea of an open centre is preserved. For a successful solution of this problem the student is referred to the example beneath the Hotel at Euston Station, London (Plate LI, Nos. IV-VI). Where possible it is better to have one large opening sufficient in width to allow two streams of

FIG. 10.   AN ITALIAN VESTIBULE WITH COVED CEILING.

traffic, and this implies guard posts and a central footway. It is important that vestibules should be designed to maintain traffic circulation and to accentuate points of axial interest in the plan of a building. Foot traffic must be guarded from the inconvenience of vehicles crossing lines of communication and adequate lighting is essential.

From experience it has been found that a square vestibule can be divided into three passage-ways over which barrel vaults, springing from intermediate colonnades form the architectural interest (Fig. 11). Several varieties of vestibule treatment are given on the Plates, and the remarks referring to elaboration of the corridor apply with equal force to the design of vestibules.

Plate XLVIII.—A three-way vestibule of simple form is shown in No. I, in which barrel vaults are supported on the side walls and from intermediate colonnades of single columns. No. II shows a variation common to Italian practice in which intersecting vaults are supported by columns, the whole area being divided into nine square compartments. In Nos. III and IV is shown the magnificent arrangement of a vestibule having the central space vaulted and the side passage-ways ceiled, found at the Farnese Palace, Rome : this is to be recommended on account of its direct simplicity and expressiveness.

Plate XLIX.—This shows the fine vestibule at Somerset House, London, and its relation to the inner halls and staircases can be seen in the key plan. Such a treatment has much to commend it from an architectural standpoint, as it is productive of fine perspective effect and the coupled columns combine strength with lightness.

Plate L.—In connection with vaulted loggias and covered ways giving access to courtyards and affording means of communication, the architecture of the outside corridor must be considered. Some suggestions for the treatment of this particular feature are given on this Plate in Nos. I to V. In general, the type follows the arcaded and vaulted loggia of Italy, and its adaptation to the plans of many kinds of modern buildings will be obvious. The student is referred to the lower storey of the buildings on the north side of the Piazza at Covent

Garden, designed by Inigo Jones, for an instance of its use when it forms an integral part of a building. The three-way vestibule beneath the central block of the Horse Guards, Whitehall, designed by William Kent (Nos. VI and VIII), partakes of the nature of the vaulted loggia and may be regarded as an early type of the vestibule with thoroughfare for wheeled traffic, which found its highest expression in the

FIG. 11. A VAULTED VESTIBULE.

work of Sir William Chambers at Somerset House, already described.

Plate LI.—This gives several examples of covered approaches for pedestrian and carriage traffic either passing through a wing of a building and leading into a courtyard or passing beneath a building from one open space to another. The general principles governing their design have already been touched upon in the introductory text to this Series.

Plates LII and LIII.—In Italy, the interiors of palace courtyards afford innumerable instances of superimposed arcaded loggias, which provide not only effective elevations but also covered communication at various levels. Repetition of the bay unit, in which single or coupled columns and piers are introduced, is the governing factor in this type of design. Such combinations of trabeation and arcuation as were evolved favoured the development of vaulted and domed ceilings, such as the beautiful example from the Vatican illustrated on Plate LII, whereas most French and English examples, which developed at a later period, were covered with flat ceilings.

REFERENCE BOOKS.

Gauthier, M. P. *Les plus Beaux Edifices de la Ville de Gênes et de ses Environs.* 1818.

Haupt, A. *Palast-Architektur, Verona.* 1908.

Letarouilly, P. M. *Edifices de Rome Moderne.* 1868.

Lowell, Guy. *Smaller Italian Villas and Farmhouses.* 1922.

Lowell, Guy. *More Small Italian Villas and Farmhouses.* 1923.

Raschdorff, J. C. *Palast-Architektur, Toscana.* 1888.

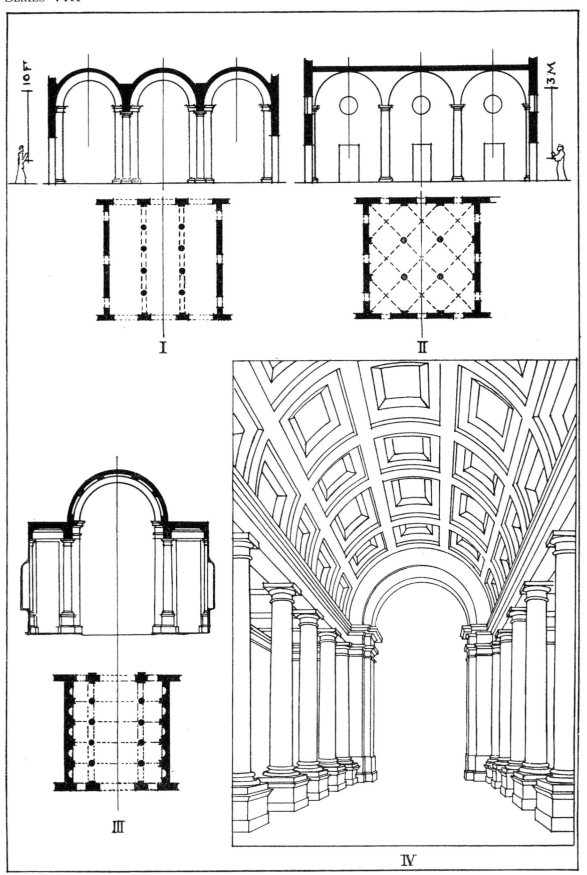

VESTIBULES AND COVERED WAYS

I-II.   GENERAL TYPES BASED ON ITALIAN PRACTICE.
III-IV.   EXAMPLE : PALAZZO FARNESE, ROME, DESIGNED BY ANTONIO SANGALLO THE YOUNGER.

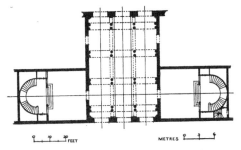

VESTIBULES AND COVERED APPROACHES

SOMERSET HOUSE, LONDON, DESIGNED BY SIR WILLIAM CHAMBERS.

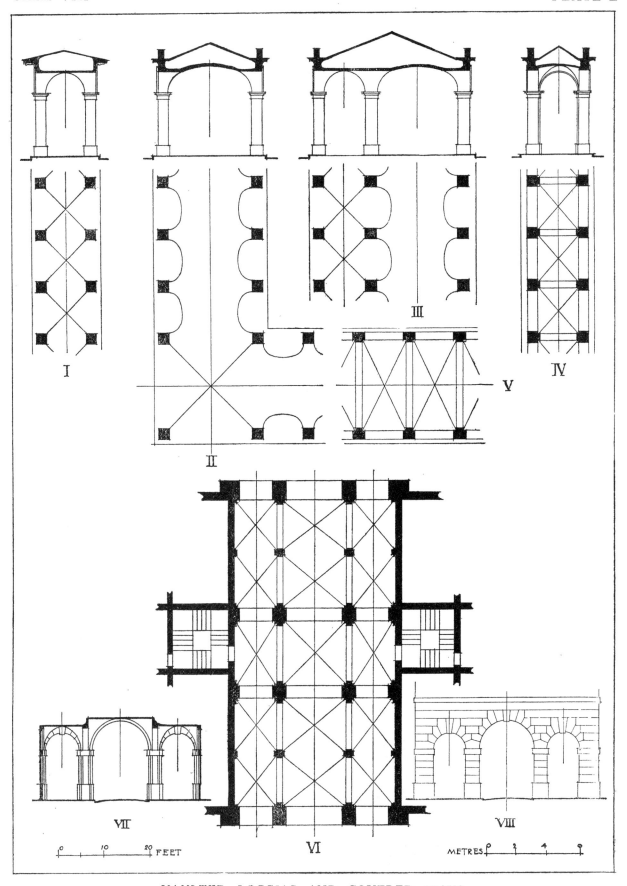

I

II

III

IV

V

VI

VII

VIII

0   10   20 FEET

METRES 0   2   4   9

VAULTED LOGGIAS AND COVERED WAYS

I-V. GENERAL TYPES BASED ON ITALIAN AND ENGLISH PRACTICE.
VI-VIII. EXAMPLE: HORSE GUARDS, WHITEHALL, LONDON, DESIGNED BY WILLIAM KENT.

PLATE LI

III

VI

VIII

II

V

IV

VII

FEET

METRES

COVERED WAYS AS CARRIAGE APPROACHES

GENERAL TYPES BASED ON ENGLISH AND FRENCH PRACTICE.

IV-VI EXAMPLE · EUSTON HOTEL, LONDON, DESIGNED BY PHILIP HARDWICK.

UPPER STORY OF ARCADED LOGGIA IN THE VATICAN

PLATE LIII

SERIES VIII

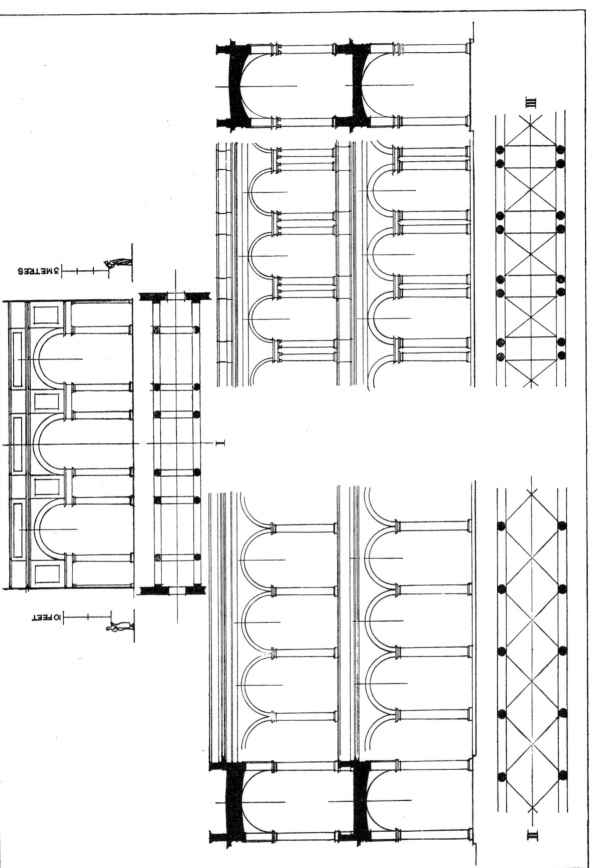

VAULTED LOGGIAS AND COVERED WAYS

GENERAL TYPES BASED ON ITALIAN SIXTEENTH AND SEVENTEENTH CENTURY PRACTICE.

I.   EXAMPLE: PALAZZO DATI, CREMONA.
II. EXAMPLE: PALAZZO CANCELLARIA, ROME, DESIGNED BY BRAMANTE.
III. EXAMPLE: PALAZZO BORGHESE, ROME, DESIGNED BY LUNGHI.

IX

STAIRCASES.

PLATES LIV TO LXV.

THE arrangement of the staircase constitutes one of the most important branches of interior design in all architectural schemes. The staircase is the principal link in a plan between two or more floors which it connects, and it must be considered equally from the standpoints of utility and beauty. The student should be acquainted with the elementary rules of staircase design and construction in various materials, and in particular be familiar with the ratio between the treads and risers in a flight so as to ensure easy " going." It is not the purpose of this Series to deal with the minute parts of staircase construction, but to show arrangements which experience has proved to be effective under certain conditions.

Staircases contained within rectangular, square, circular and elliptical compartments are included, with a variety of treatments especially suited to the particular plan form, but no attempt has been made to show exceptional dispositions of flights which are often more remarkable for their ingenuity than for the impressiveness and directness of result. Types have been selected from many well-known buildings, and architectural detail has only been suggested in order that the underlying principles can be the more readily grasped.

Three factors determine the position of a staircase in a plan : first, its situation in regard to the principal apartments ; secondly, the desirability of preserving axial communication free from obstruction ; and thirdly, the necessity of providing adequate lighting not only to the staircase but also along adjacent corridors, vestibules and other communications, the staircase acting as a " well " for the distribution of light. The examples chosen for illustration fulfil these conditions in-so-far as they are considered as isolated motives. Every opportunity should be taken of studying this important feature *in situ*, and buildings should be visited in order to appreciate first-hand the possibilities of staircase design.

Plates LIV and LV.—Nearly every building of civic importance lends itself to monumental treatment internally, and the staircase whether designed as an introductory feature to a series of apartments or as a means of ascent to a principal floor should be so arranged as to impress at once by its scale and spaciousness. The examples shown on these and the three succeeding Plates have been selected to illustrate some of the dispositions best calculated to convey an imposing effect when used for grand staircases in public buildings.   On Plate LV, No. I, is the plan of a central flight staircase arranged in an open hall giving direct access to a first floor with galleries returning at the sides and open corridors below.   This form permits of similar flights being placed underneath in a parallel direction for access to a basement.   In No. II the staircase is contained between side walls and is calculated to give the maximum effect of strength and dignity.   The returning corridors at the first floor level are screened by means of columns resting upon the enclosing side walls : the famous staircase at the Luxembourg, Paris, erected under the régime of Napoleon, of which a perspective sketch is reproduced on Plate LIV, is perhaps the best example of this treatment.   No. III shows the plan of a direct staircase of two parallel flights built upon solid walls forming an open access at the ground floor level : it is useful in connection with plans requiring the central approach to be kept open. No. IV shows plan and section of a monumental staircase arranged on either side of a central hall with subsidiary corridors on the ground floor and galleries over them : the central hall being ceiled at the first floor level.   The perspective of such an arrangement admits of excellent possibilities architecturally, such as the introduction of barrel vaults for top-lighting, domes and semi-domes.   No. V shows the adaptation of No. III duplicated on either side of a central vestibule.

Plate LVI.—A " dog-leg " staircase, placed off a corridor with ample space for landings, is shown in No. I : this represents the simplest type of staircase with " returned " flights.   In No. II is shown an extension of the theory of the " dog-leg " arrangement, with the addition of a small open space or " well " between the flights, a preferable arrangement to be followed whenever permitted by the width of the staircase.   A three-way staircase is given in No. III, the central flight being the main ascent from the ground floor to the first landing, whence parallel returned flights rise on either side.   It is desirable in a staircase of this type to make the width of the lower flight slightly greater than that of the upper ones : this triple form is useful when a dignified approach is required on a small scale.   No. IV shows the principle of No. I applied on either side of a central vestibule, and No. V shows the adaptation of type No. III with the addition of either large or small " well " openings between the flights, the vista from the vestibulte being directed to the enclosing walls of the staircase.   This arrangement, as seen in the section No. VI, admits of the introduction of a large central top-lighted landing giving access to suites of apartments on the upper level in two directions.   Such a disposition is eminently suited to buildings in which architectural display is desirable.

Plate LVII.—The treatment shown in diagrams Nos. I and II is in principle an extension of the theories illustrated in diagrams Nos. IV and V on Plate LV.

In this case, however, the staircase is continued to the full width of the central space with columns forming screens at the junction of the staircase with the vestibule on the ground floor, and an internal peristyle completing the architectural sequence above. Nos. III and IV show a highly successful grouping of twin staircases on either side of a circular vestibule. In this case it has been possible to light the staircases only from above, but such is the ingenuity of the design that every part is adequately lit. These diagrams are based on the internal approaches at Drury Lane Theatre, London, which have been in continual use for a century. In this building not only was it necessary for the public to reach the first floor level in a direct manner, but access to a higher level was essential, and this was affected by diminishing the width of the upper flight, thereby obstructing the flow of light from above as little as possible. This example should be of great interest to the student for, on analysis, it will be found that in the arrangement are combined many of the elemental forms described in preceding series of Plates in this book, such as the combination of circles, squares, columnar screens, coved ceilings and domes, and he will observe the importance of the fact that in all such compositions, if they are to be successful, one feature must dominate both vertically and horizontally.

Plate LVIII.—The example illustrated in the plan, section and perspective sketch on this Plate has been taken from the admirable design for the grand staircase of the Federal Palace in Mexico City. It is without question one of the most stately compositions ever designed and is noteworthy on account of its direct simplicity. The two broad staircases are arranged in lofty halls on either side of a central vestibule, a treatment which admits of the open circulation being preserved without check at all levels, and allows of the maximum effect of spaciousness. Such grandeur is only suitable for buildings of the first rank where large assemblies meet and where civic and semi-state functions are performed.

Plate LIX.—These perspective sketches show two-way staircases approached from a preliminary central flight on the axial line. The plan of the upper example from Dodington House, Gloucestershire, is similar in principle to that given in No. I, Plate LX: on the same Plate the plan of the lower example from the Athenæum Club, London, is given in Nos. III and IV.

Plate LX.—These plans are based upon existing motives in which the staircase becomes a feature extraneous to a vestibule or hall approach, carrying on the architectural treatment and completing the vista. It will be seen that provision for lighting either from the top or from the end wall has been one of the governing conditions of these designs.

Plate LXI.—The plan and perspective sketch, No. 1, illustrate the main staircase at the British Museum, London, which is notable for its monumental treatment. It is arranged in three flights, the central or approach flight being twice the width of the " return " flights. This staircase is successful on account of the sense of solidity and support given to the parts, and it affords a valuable motive that should be noted by the student.

It is sometimes necessary to introduce a staircase as a feature in a large public waiting hall which must not encroach too much on the floor space. A staircase in direct flights would not fulfil this condition. The interesting example in the Great Hall at Euston Station, London, designed by Philip Hardwick, shown in No. II, is an ingenious arrangement, suggested by Italian precedent; it is at once functional and architectural, for it lends dignity to the scale of the hall and does not encroach unduly upon the floor space.

Plate LXII.—The diagrams on this Plate represent motives for square staircases with flights returned in each case. No. I shows the simplest type with short flights and quarter-space landings. No. II is larger in its dimensions, the flights being carried on walls and screened by columns which in turn support the covering over the well, in which a top-light is formed. In No. III the staircase is designed about an open well and is contained within a square, round which circulating corridors, screened by columns, complete the design. No. IV shows a staircase of three flights only, arranged about a central well, the fourth side of the square being taken up by the landing. No. V shows a staircase with returned flights arranged within an open square. The staircase shown in plan No. VI and perspective sketch No. VII consists of three flights placed against the sides of a square hall. It is partially screened by a colonnade upon which other columns are superimposed at the first floor level: this is an effective arrangement admitting of correct emphasis being given to the first floor approach.

Plates LXIII and LXIV.—The circular staircase on a large scale is rarely adopted for more than one or two flights, as it is primarily of use in connection with the design of a rotunda which itself is but an incident in a grandiose scheme. The diagrams Nos. I, II and III show circular staircases rising from one or more floors, Sir Christopher Wren's geometrical staircase in St. Paul's Cathedral, No. II, being unique as regards the number of steps, daring construction, masterly design of the lower flight and diminished width of the upper flights. No. IV shows short flights adapted at three points in the design of a rotunda, giving access to a circular corridor and subsidiary passages, and at the same time leading to a central flight of steps at the head of the vista. The plan and section given in Nos. V and VI show a variation of the principles illustrated in No. IV. A segmental flight is disposed between the podium of a circular peristyle and continued by a straight flight on the main axis beyond the circular plan. In these examples the student will recognise an extension of some of the circular domed motives which have been discussed in Series I of this book, and an interesting composition which includes curved steps and screens within a circular domed building is reproduced on Plate LIV.

The treatment of the top landing calls for rare skill in the adjustment of peristyles, domical coverings and lantern lights. The use of a dome is readily suggested by the ring of columns in the example from Wardour Castle, illustrated on Plate LXIII, but even over a rectangular plan the domical covering may be relied upon to give excellent results, as may be judged from the other perspective sketch reproduced on the same Plate.

Plate LXV.—The design of semi-circular and elliptical staircases formed a departure in late Renaissance practice in all parts of Europe and provided innumerable examples from which a few of the diagrams shown on this Plate have been drawn. No. I is a treatment admitting of an open staircase with a straight central flight and geometrical returned flights in two directions, leading to a spacious first floor landing indicated on the plan : subsidiary service stairs are ingeniously combined on either side. No. II is a scheme for a geometrical staircase occupying a semi-circular space and having returned curved flights. A screen of columns, introduced at the ground floor level to mark the line of the corridor, gives distinction to the design and carries a broad landing at the first floor level, the light balustrading of the staircase being continued between the returned flights. The lighting for a staircase of this type can be arranged either from the side walls or from a lantern light sympathetic to the shape of the well. In the design shown in No. III the staircase is placed in an ellipse with direct lighting : the service staircases being placed in turrets on either side of the axial line. This example offers suggestions for design in country houses where the staircase is used as a prominent feature of the interior and where it occupies a position demanding external expression. An extension of the theory of the elliptical well is seen in No. IV, where the well is screened from the staircase by the superimposition of coupled columns which are structural features. No. V shows a simple three-way staircase occupying an ellipse. A grandiose conception is shown in No. VI in which the staircase is placed in an elliptical well having a short central flight with returns : a circulating corridor is carried all round the staircase and screened from the well by a peristyle. Semi-circular recesses are introduced in the outer corners, formed by enclosing the elliptical plan within a rectangle, and the spaces in the inner corners are given up to the service staircases. Such a staircase could not be successfully introduced for more than one storey in height, but wherever conditions demand particular attention to internal architectural effect an arrangement of this kind offers many possibilities. In the small example shown in No. VII the staircase runs round an elliptical well in one direction only, all the steps being curved. From the standpoint of both utility and beauty this simple arrangement has much to commend it. No. VIII shows an adaptation of the principle of No. VII under slightly different conditions : these two examples admit of lighting either from the side or from the top.

REFERENCE BOOKS

Britton and Pugin. *Illustrations of the Public Buildings of London.* 1825-28.

Cloquet, L. *Traité d'Architecture.* 1898-1901.   Vol. II.

Durand, J. N. L. *Précis des Léçons d'Architecture.* 1802-9.

Guadet. *Eléments et Theorie de l'Architecture.* 1904. Vols. I and V.

Krafft, J., et Ransonette, N. *Plans . . . des plus belles Maisons et des Hotels à Paris.* 1771-1802.

Letarouilly, P. M. *Edifices de Rome Moderne.* 1868.

Richardson, G. *The New Vitruvius Britannicus.* 1802-8.

FIG. 12. STAIRCASE IN THE PALAZZO BALBI, GENOA.

PLATE LIV

II. COMPOSITION BY PIRANESI

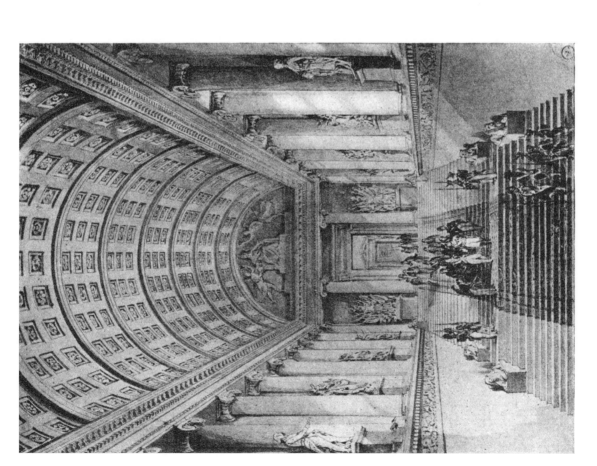

I. MONUMENTAL STAIRCASE: LUXEMBOURG, PARIS

PLATE LV

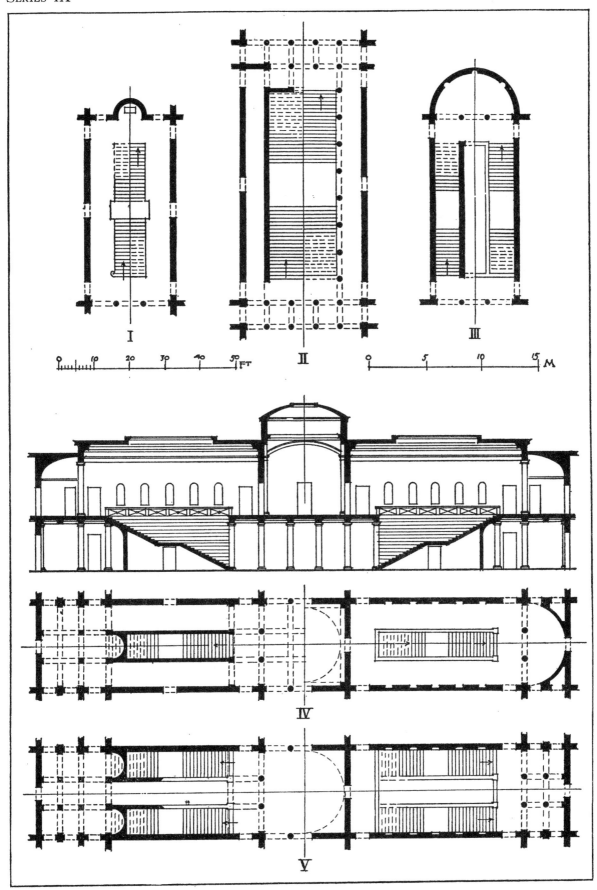

INTERNAL STAIRCASES WITH "STRAIGHT" FLIGHTS

I-V. GENERAL TYPES.

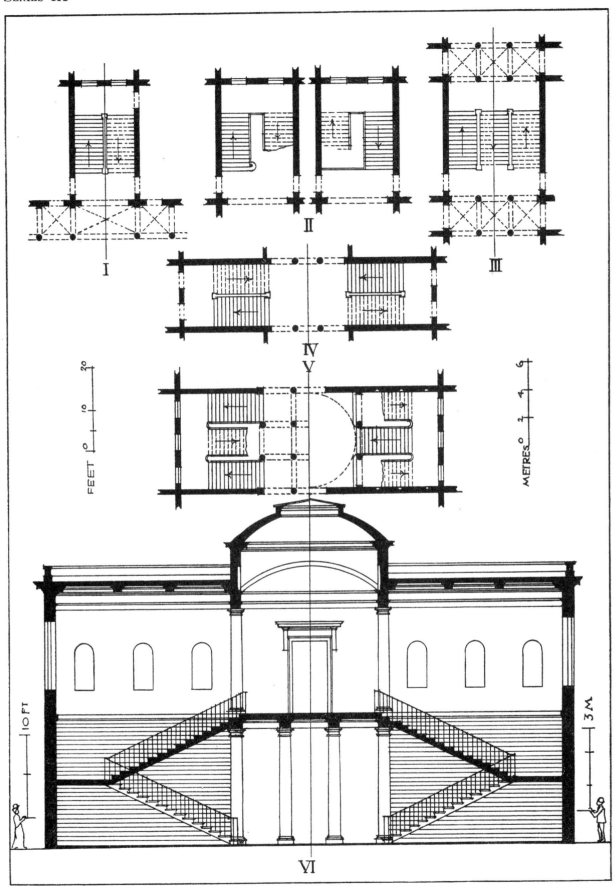

FEET

METRES

10 FT

3 M

I   II   III   IV   V   VI

INTERNAL STAIRCASES WITH "RETURNED" FLIGHTS

I-VI.   GENERAL TYPES.

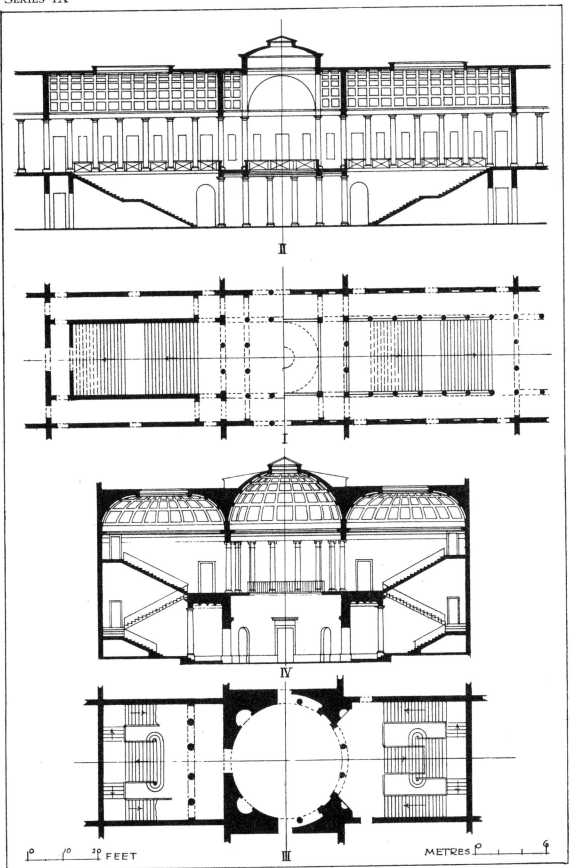

II

I

IV

0   10   20 FEET   METRES 0   1   2

III

STAIRCASES WITH CENTRAL DOMED HALLS

I-II.   "STRAIGHT" FLIGHTS, SHOWING AN EXTENSION OF THE PRINCIPLES ILLUSTRATED IN NOS. IV. AND V., PLATE LV.
III-IV. "RETURNED" FLIGHTS, SHOWING AN EXTENSION OF THE PRINCIPLES ILLUSTRATED IN NOS. V. AND VI., PLATE LVI.
EXAMPLE: DRURY LANE THEATRE, DESIGNED BY BENJAMIN WYATT.

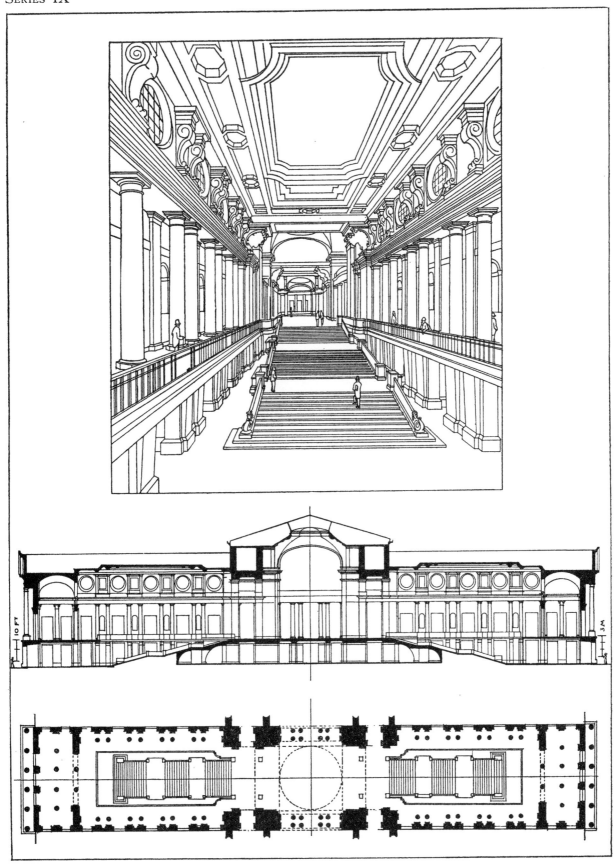

MONUMENTAL STAIRCASE WITH "STRAIGHT" FLIGHTS

EXAMPLE: THE FEDERAL PALACE, MEXICO CITY, DESIGNED BY F. BÉNARD.

TWO-WAY STAIRCASE WITH PRELIMINARY CENTRAL FLIGHT

I.   DODINGTON HOUSE, GLOUCESTERSHIRE, DESIGNED BY JAMES WYATT.

II.   THE ATHENAEUM CLUB, LONDON, DESIGNED BY DECIMUS BURTON.

(See Plate LX, Nos. III and IV, for plans of this staircase)

PLATE LX

SERIES IX

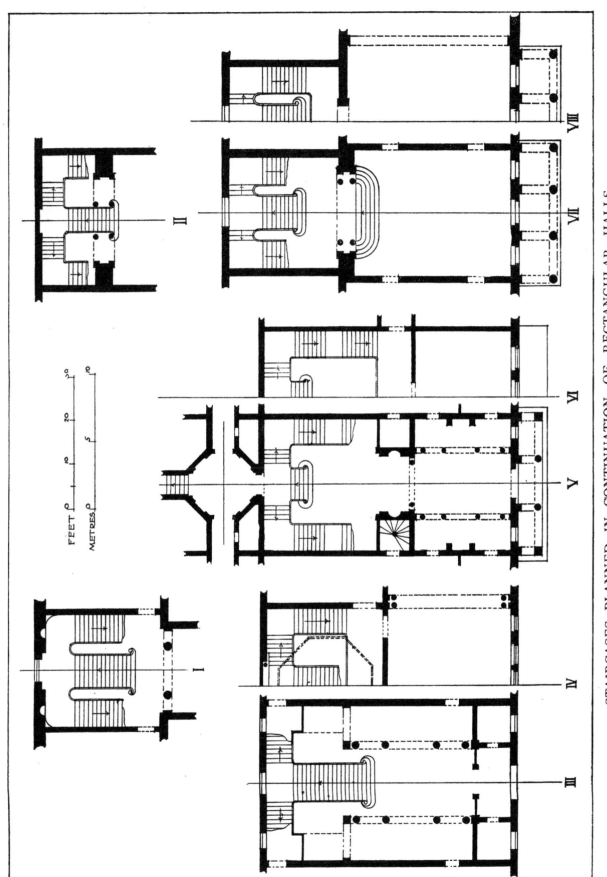

STAIRCASES PLANNED IN CONTINUATION OF RECTANGULAR HALLS

GENERAL TYPES BASED ON EIGHTEENTH CENTURY PRACTICE IN ENGLAND AND FRANCE.

(See also *Plate LIX*)

III-IV. EXAMPLE: ATHENAEUM CLUB, LONDON, DESIGNED BY DECIMUS BURTON.
V-VI. EXAMPLE: THE LONDON INSTITUTION, DESIGNED BY WILLIAM BROOKS.

FEET
METRES

PLATE LXI

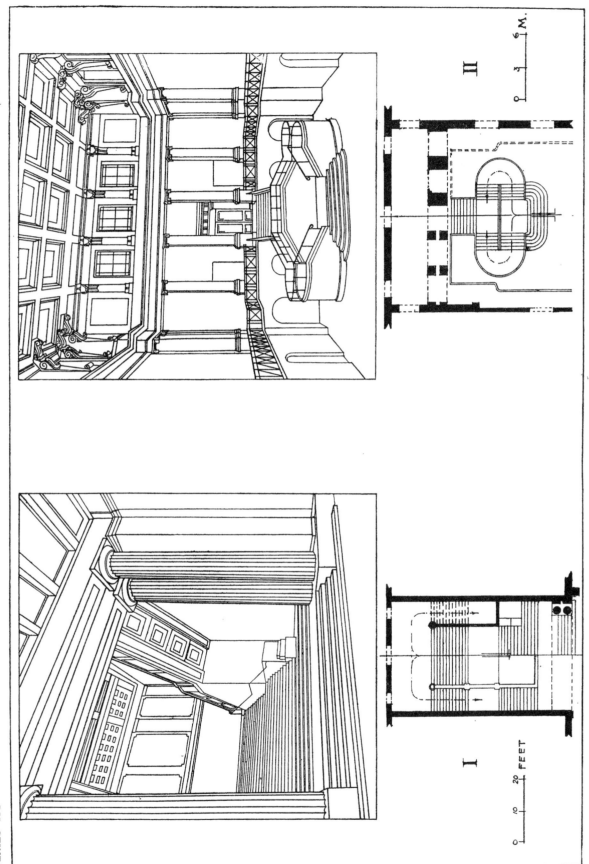

II

0   3   6 M.

I

0   10   20 FEET

MONUMENTAL STAIRCASES WITH "RETURNED" FLIGHTS

I. EXAMPLE: BRITISH MUSEUM, LONDON, DESIGNED BY SIR ROBERT SMIRKE.
II. EXAMPLE: GREAT HALL, EUSTON STATION, LONDON, DESIGNED BY P. HARDWICK.

PLATE LXII

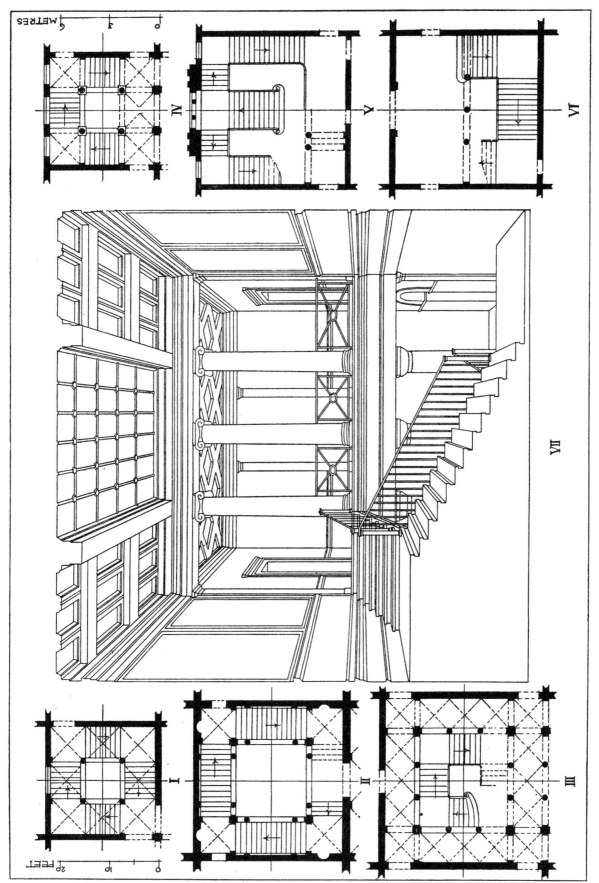

STAIRCASES WITH "RETURNED" FLIGHTS PLANNED WITHIN A SQUARE

I-IV.   GENERAL TYPES BASED ON ITALIAN PRACTICE.
V.   EXAMPLE: BOOTHAM SCHOOL, YORK.
VI-VII.   PLAN AND PERSPECTIVE SKETCH AFTER CHATEAUNEUF.

STAIRCASES WITH DOMICAL CEILINGS

I. WARDOUR CASTLE, WILTSHIRE, DESIGNED BY JAMES PAINE. FROM AN ORIGINAL DRAWING BY J. C. BUCKLER.
(See Plate LXIV, No. III, for plan)

II. SELWOOD PARK, BERKSHIRE, DESIGNED BY ROBERT MITCHELL.

PLATE LXIV

SERIES IX

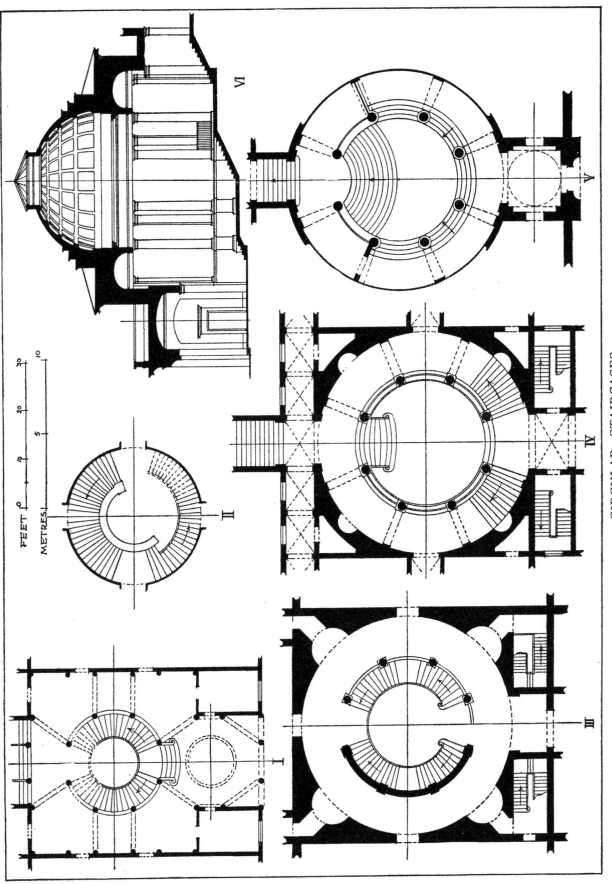

CIRCULAR STAIRCASES

GENERAL TYPES BASED ON FRENCH AND ENGLISH PRACTICE.
III. EXAMPLE : WARDOUR CASTLE, WILTSHIRE, DESIGNED BY JAMES PAINE.
V-VI. EXAMPLE : DOVER HOUSE, WHITEHALL, DESIGNED BY HENRY HOLLAND.

FEET
METRES

PLATE LXV

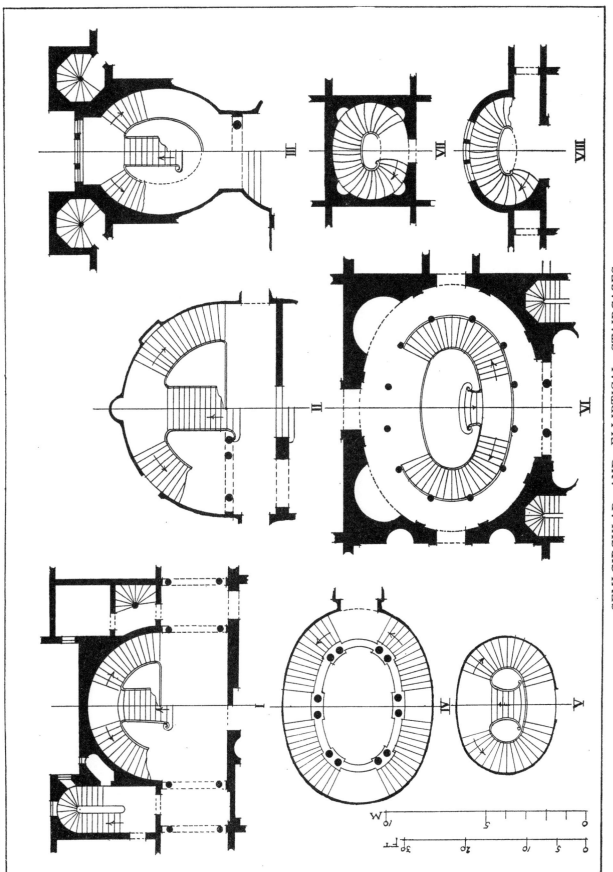

SEMI-CIRCULAR AND ELLIPTICAL STAIRCASES

GENERAL TYPES FROM ENGLISH, FRENCH AND ITALIAN EIGHTEENTH CENTURY PRACTICE.

I. EXAMPLE: TRINITY HOUSE, LONDON, DESIGNED BY JAMES WYATT.
II. EXAMPLE: WENTWORTH WOODHOUSE, YORKSHIRE, DESIGNED BY CARR, OF YORK.
VI. EXAMPLE: CULZEAN CASTLE, N.B., DESIGNED BY THE BROTHERS ADAM.

X

PAVILIONS, LOGGIAS AND OPEN HALLS.

PLATES LXVI TO LXVIII.

AMONG the problems of the present day which are likely to be encountered by the designer, that of the outdoor pavilion and the covered space, open on all sides, must be considered. At all periods this particular form of building has produced a variety of types which in principle are closely related. To name a few instances of its purpose: it is applicable to the arrangement of architectural schemes in public and private parks: it has been found essential for market-places and civic centres: it can be modified to serve as a street shelter, and it can form the entrance to a railway station, while many other uses will readily suggest themselves.

The pavilion or loggia can also be applied to form a portico, as in the case of the Italian villa, or it may be used as a projecting porte-cochère or as any other architectural feature designed to mark the centre of a building. In the above-mentioned cases, the loggia or porch can follow either the accepted arcuated models of Italy or more severe classic lines.

Apart from the well-known examples at Abingdon, Berkshire; Poole, Dorsetshire; and Peterborough, Northamptonshire, all of which form basement storeys of market halls, the single storey pavilion or covered space is peculiarly suited to the needs of a market. The market at Taunton, Somersetshire, is a case in point, and the old market shelter at St. Albans, Hertfordshire (no longer existing), as well as the wooden pavilion designed by Bell which in the eighteenth century formed the chief attraction of the " Tuesday Market Place " at King's Lynn, Norfolk, indicate the direction in which the imagination of the designer can be safely guided.

For more elaborate versions, reference can be made to the markets designed by Charles Fowler at Exeter and Covent Garden, London: the smaller markets at Paris and the older types abounding in the cities of Italy.

Plate LXVI.—On this Plate various types of open halls are shown, all pre-eminently suited to the design of market and other shelters.

151

Plate LXVII.—This gives examples of isolated pavilions or loggias, both simple and Palladian, which can be considered either as independent features complete in themselves, or as forming incidents in larger compositions.

Plate LXVIII.—These designs are suitable for pavilions standing alone in open spaces. No. III partakes also of the nature of a gateway.

REFERENCE BOOKS.

Bruyère, L. *Etudes relatives à L'Art des Constructions.* 1823-28.

Canina, L. *L'Architettura Antica.* 1839-40.

Gourlier. *Choix d'Edifices, Publics Projetés et Construits en France Depuis le Commencement du XIXme Siècle.* 1825-36.

Lowell, Guy. *Smaller Italian Villas and Farmhouses.* 1922.

Percier, C., et Fontaine, P. *Choix des plus Cèlebrès Maisons de Plaisance de Rome et ses Environs.* 1824.

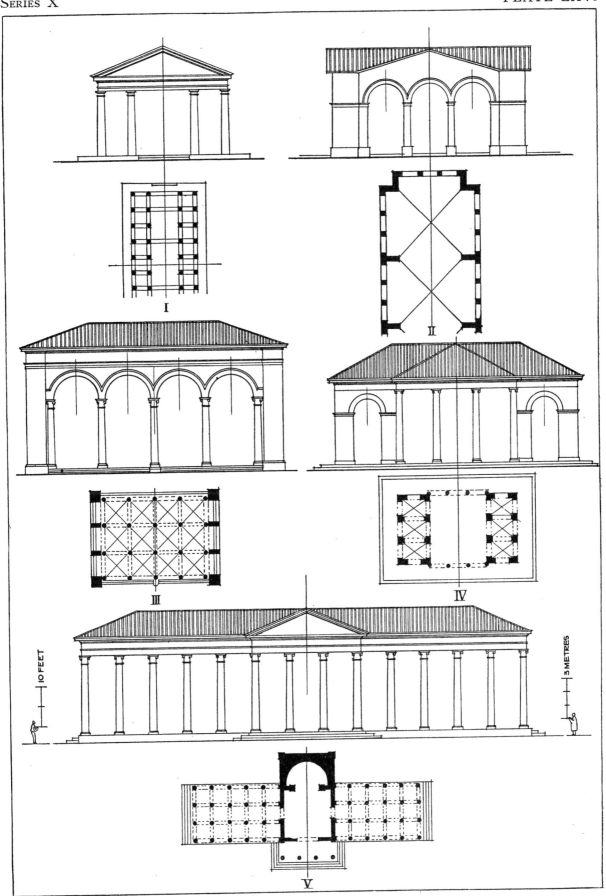

I

II

III

IV

10 FEET

3 METRES

V

PAVILIONS OPEN ON ALL SIDES

GENERAL TYPES FROM ROMAN AND RENAISSANCE PRACTICE.

III.   EXAMPLE : THE MERCATO NUOVO, FLORENCE, DESIGNED BY BERNARDO TASSO.

IV.   EXAMPLE : THE MARKET HOUSE, LIMERICK.

PLATE LXVII

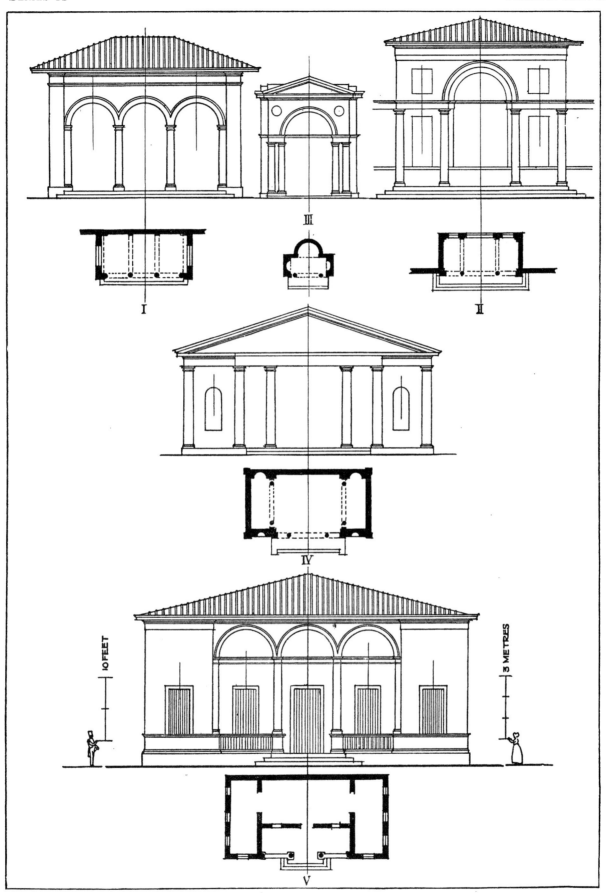

ISOLATED PAVILIONS OR LOGGIAS

I-V.   GENERAL TYPES BASED ON ENGLISH AND ITALIAN EIGHTEENTH CENTURY PRACTICE.

PLATE LXVIII

SERIES X

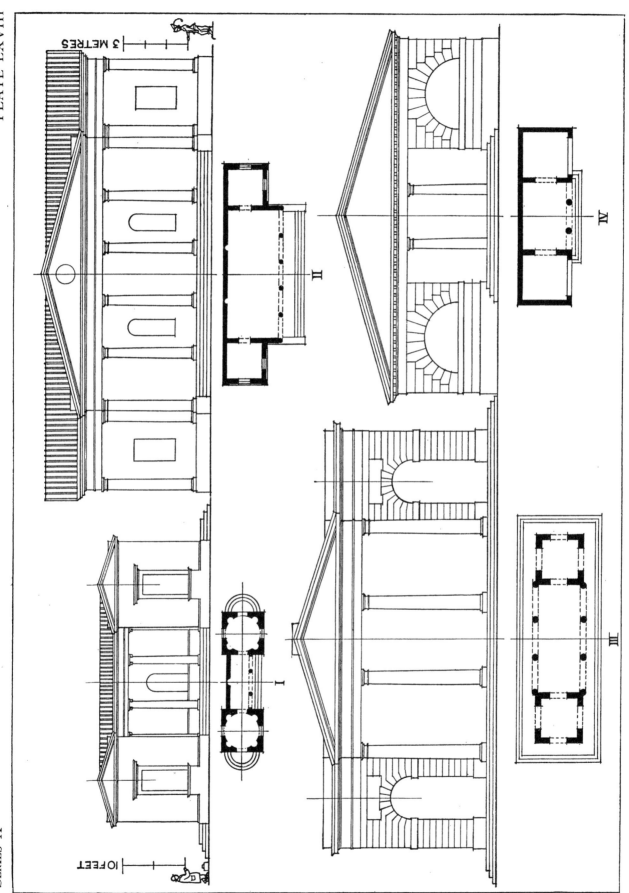

3 METRES

10 FEET

II

I

IV

III

ISOLATED PAVILIONS OR LOGGIAS

I-IV.   GENERAL TYPES BASED ON ENGLISH AND FRENCH EIGHTEENTH CENTURY PRACTICE.

XI

FACADES.

PLATES LXIX TO LXXXV.

THIS series aims at analysing the component parts of buildings of not more than two principal storeys in height and of limited dimensions. The elevations illustrated on the Plates have been chosen arbitrarily, for no fixed rules can be laid down for determining the design of façades. In all good design the plan finds expression externally, and features subordinate to the general outline of a building are in direct relation to the plan. The examples selected have been taken for the most part from existing buildings, but they have been supplemented by a certain number of unexecuted designs preserved in National and private collections. Most of them are very simple in arrangement, and care has been taken to present only designs which contain elements, both functional and logical, such as can be adapted to the purposes of modern buildings similar in size and character. Study of the Plates in other sections of this book will show that a great variety of façades can be obtained, other than those shown, by using any of the accepted geometrical plan forms, with their individual elevations, to form points of interest in a composition. The arrangement of an entrance or a portico in relation to the spacing of voids and solids; the introduction of arcuated features, such as are afforded by the " Palladian " motive; the loggia, projecting or recessed; and the vertical feature of large scale used to contrast with the general horizontality of a façade, are all instances of the scope left to the judgment of the individual. Other considerations, equally vital, but of the nature of refinements, concern the proportions of vertical and horizontal fenestration; the need for diminishing the height and width of window openings in superimposed storeys; and the massing of openings to form sub-groupings of the main composition in order to enhance the breadth of a façade that is entirely free from breaks.

Novel suggestions will be obtained by the analysis of façades into their main and secondary masses, apart from the question of subsidiary features. Some of those illustrated consist of a single mass, having the sub-motives arranged as focal points to contrast in a decorative sense with the general mass (Plates LXIX-LXXVII): some are formed of three masses, a main centre with two symmetrical wings; while others rely for their effect upon the main masses on either side of an axial line with a connecting link between them (Plate LXXVIII). Some of the schemes, based upon pavilions and loggias (Plate LXXIX), have been selected to include the treatment of terraces and steps which lend so much charm to their correct setting amidst natural surroundings.

The treatment of façades in the streets of cities, when the frontages become in effect intra-mural galleries, such as the three world-famed examples, the Palazzo Uffizi by Vasari, in Florence ; the Rue de Rivoli, Paris, by Percier and Fontaine ; and the Regent Street Quadrant, London, by Nash, as originally built, point to the advisability of simple repetition for street architecture on a large scale.   Many thoroughfares in London and other cities which in the eighteenth and early nineteenth centuries were lined with façades, in which continuity of the main horizontal lines is preserved, may also be cited for the quiet dignity that distinguishes them irrespective of the materials employed.

Façades with more than two main horizontal sub-divisions are illustrated in Plate LXXXIV, and the proportioning of the horizontal masses should be especially noted.   In No. I, taken from the Bank of England at Liverpool, the façade is divided horizontally into two main parts, the larger distribution being given to the lower storey.   The example given in No. IV, from the Wellington Street front of Somerset House, London, consists of three horizontal sub-divisions, of which the larger is the middle storey.   The law governing the rhythmic grouping of masses in a vertical direction also applies to the horizontal sub-division of masses : experience will enable the student to grasp this principle and to apply it to any problems he may be called upon to solve.

In the past, before distinctions were drawn between engineering and architecture, the design of bridges came within the province of the architect.   Apart from the question of bridges as features of town development, the bridge motive gives opportunities in the arrangement of architectural masses, the " Palladian " loggias on the river front of Somerset House (Plate LXXXV) being a case in point, where the bridge and the loggia connect two blocks of a building in such a way as to allow of a vista to the courtyard with open access below.   There are also certain well-known examples of open screens above the span of a bridge to connect adjacent buildings : for instance, the bridge which carries Princes Street to the Calton Hill, Edinburgh, illustrated on the same Plate.

The varieties of expression that can be given to elevations depend upon extraneous circumstances, so that it is almost impossible to formulate definite rules for their treatment.   The best examples of the past, particularly those of the eighteenth century, while showing restraint no less than the limitations imposed by the general acceptance of the classic ideal, do not present a very wide range of composition.   Mere repetition of these well-known themes does not satisfy the demand for greater freedom in external expression which arises from the prevailing impulse for truth and reality in building.   At the present time, however, it would be unwise to direct the attention of students to types of design which are purely experimental, and the main purpose of this book is to ensure that intelligent evolution shall be encouraged in preference to fantastic adventure.

REFERENCE BOOKS.

ENGLISH :

Belcher and Macartney. *Later Renaissance Architecture in England.* 1897-1901.

Field, N., and Bunney, M. *English Domestic Architecture of the Seventeenth and Eighteenth Centuries.* 1905.

Ramsey, S., and Harvey, J. D. M. *Small Houses of the Late Georgian Period,* 1923.

Richardson, A. E. *Monumental Architecture in Great Britain.*

FRENCH :

Krafft, J., and Ransonette, N. *Plans . . des plus belles Maisons et Hotels . . à Paris.* 1771-1802.

Gourlier. *Choix d'Edifices Publics.* 1825-36.

Le Doux, C. N. *L'Architecture Consideré sous le Rapport de l'Art.* 1804.

ITALIAN :

Cicognara, L. *Fabbriche e i Monumenti Conspicui di Venezia.* 1838-40.

Lowell, Guy. *Smaller Italian Villas and Farmhouses.* 1922.

Lowell, Guy. *More Small Italian Villas and Farmhouses.* 1923.

Scheult, F. L. *Recueil d'Architecture.* 1821.

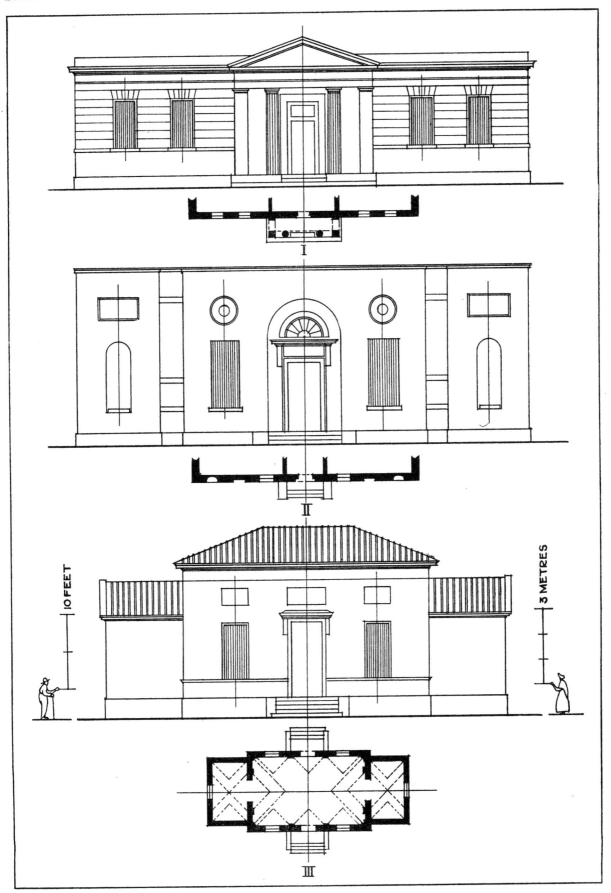

FACADES ONE PRINCIPAL STOREY IN HEIGHT

I.   EXAMPLE: THE OLD BATHS, ILFRACOMBE, DEVONSHIRE.
II. EXAMPLE: WINGS OF THE RADCLIFFE OBSERVATORY, OXFORD, DESIGNED BY HENRY KEENE.
III. GENERAL TYPE, CIRCA 1800.

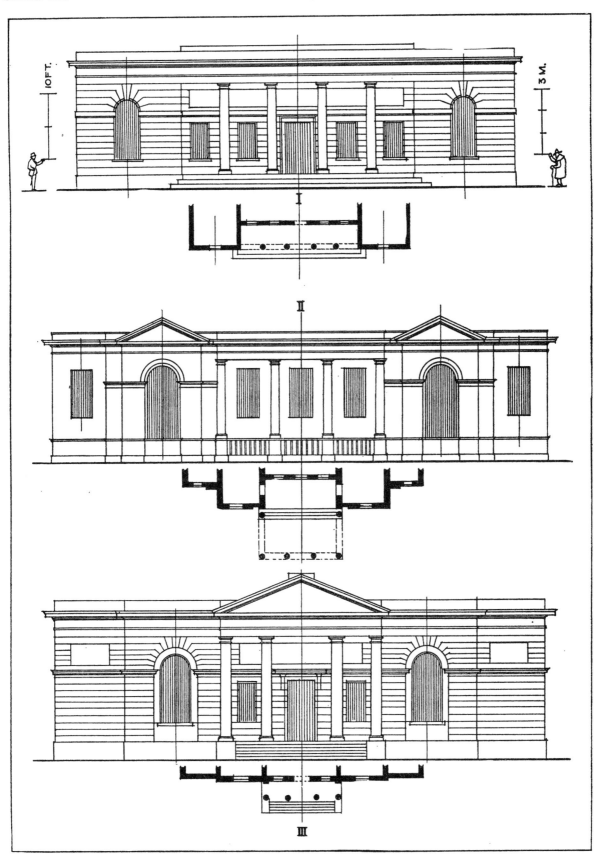

FACADES ONE PRINCIPAL STOREY IN HEIGHT

GENERAL TYPE CIRCA 1800. II. EXAMPLE: ARLINGTON STREET, LONDON.
III. EXAMPLE: RUSSELL INSTITUTION, LONDON, NO LONGER EXISTING.

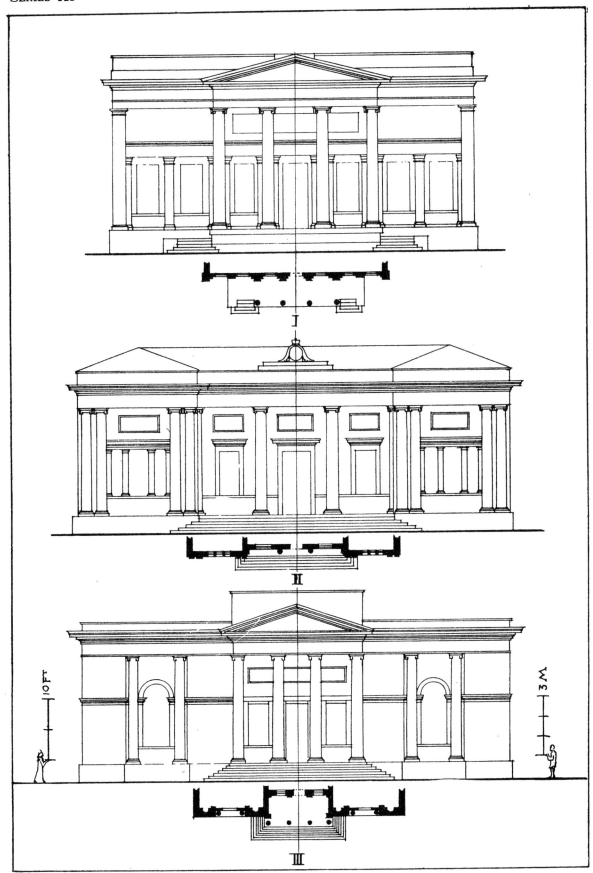

FACADES ONE PRINCIPAL STOREY IN HEIGHT

I-III.   GENERAL TYPES BASED ON LATE EIGHTEENTH CENTURY PRACTICE IN ENGLAND.

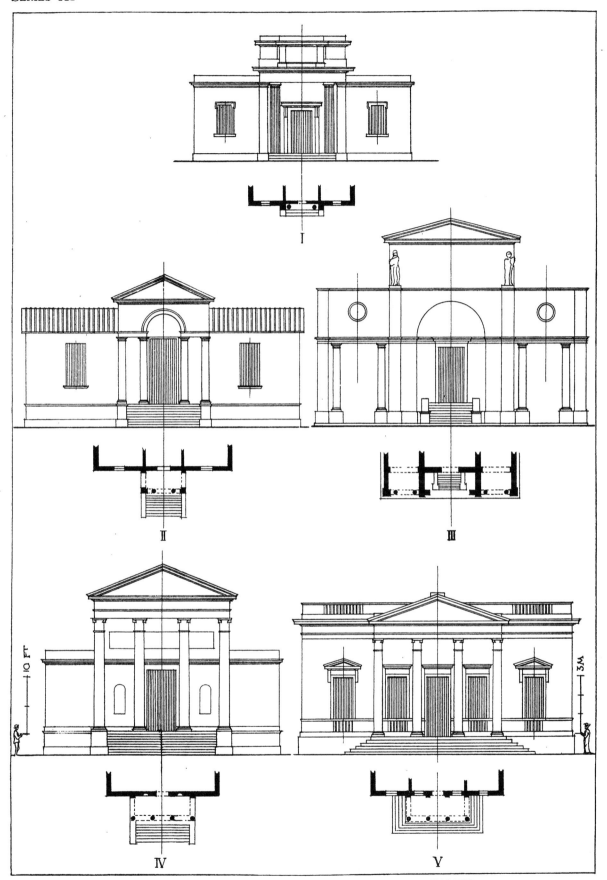

FACADES ONE PRINCIPAL STOREY IN HEIGHT

I.   EXAMPLE : LODGE, HYDE PARK, LONDON, DESIGNED BY DECIMUS BURTON.
II·III.   GENERAL TYPES BASED ON SEVENTEENTH CENTURY ITALIAN PRACTICE.
IV·V.   GENERAL TYPES BASED ON EIGHTEENTH CENTURY ENGLISH PRACTICE.

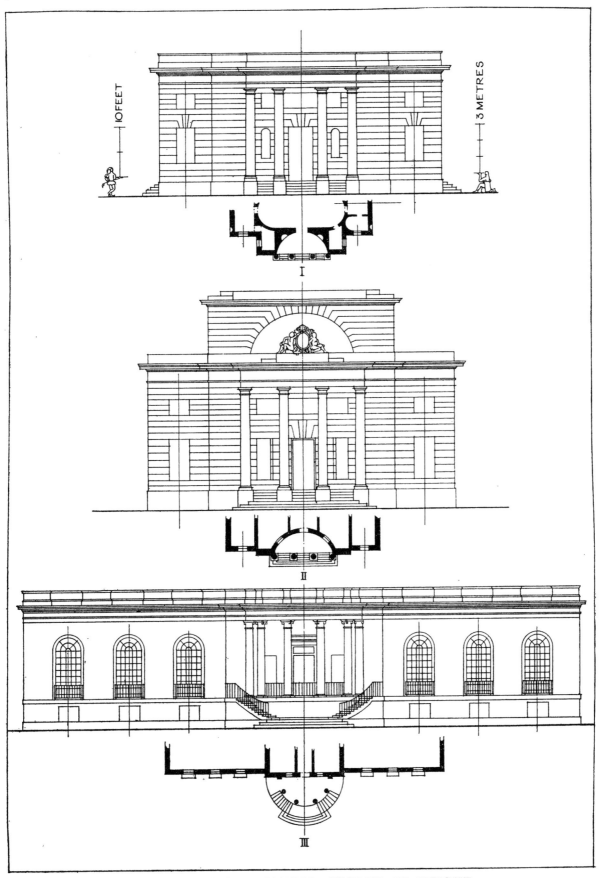

IO FEET

3 METRES

I

II

III

FACADES ONE PRINCIPAL STOREY IN HEIGHT

I·II.   WITH RECESSED SEMI-CIRCULAR PORCHES, AFTER LE DOUX.

III.   WITH PROJECTING SEMI-CIRCULAR PORCH.   EXAMPLE : LIBRARY, WALTHAM, MASS., U.S.A., DESIGNED BY MESSRS. LORING AND LELAND.

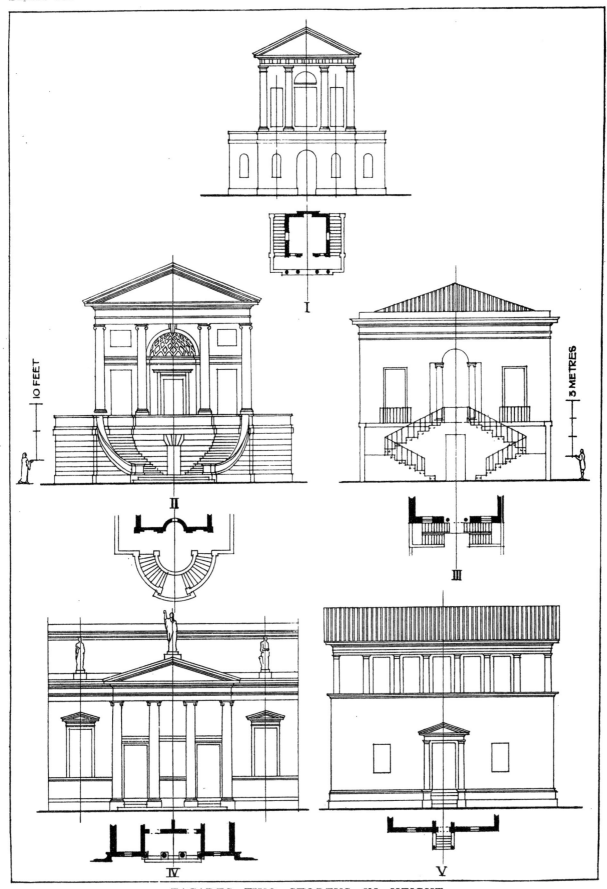

FACADES TWO STOREYS IN HEIGHT

GENERAL TYPES BASED ON ENGLISH, FRENCH AND ITALIAN PRACTICE.

I-II. DESIGNS BY PAUL SANDBY, PRESERVED IN SIR JOHN SOANE'S MUSEUM.

IV. EXAMPLE: COMMERCIAL ROOMS, BRISTOL, DESIGNED BY JOHN LINNELL BOND

PLATE LXXV

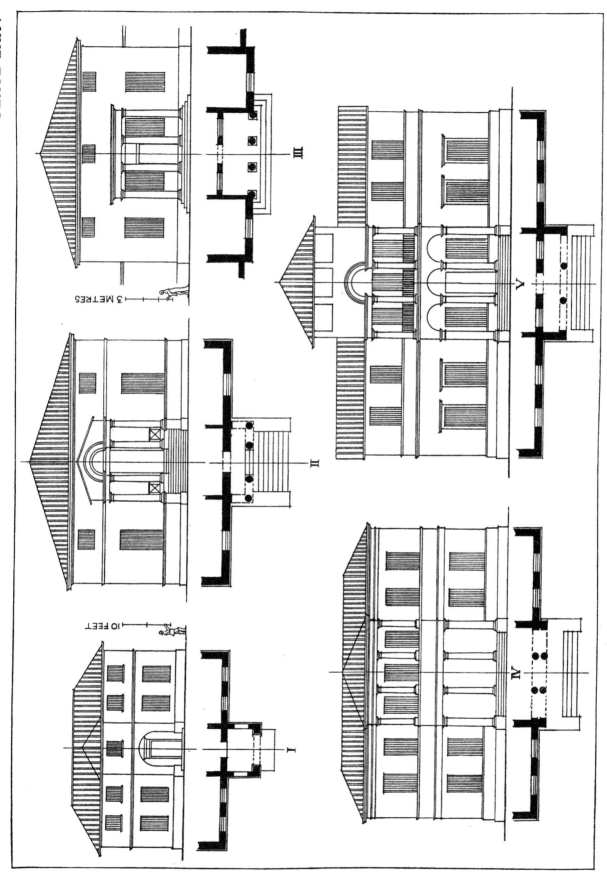

3 METRES

10 FEET

III

II

V

IV

I

FACADES TWO STOREYS IN HEIGHT

I-V. GENERAL TYPES BASED ON ITALIAN AND FRENCH PRACTICE.

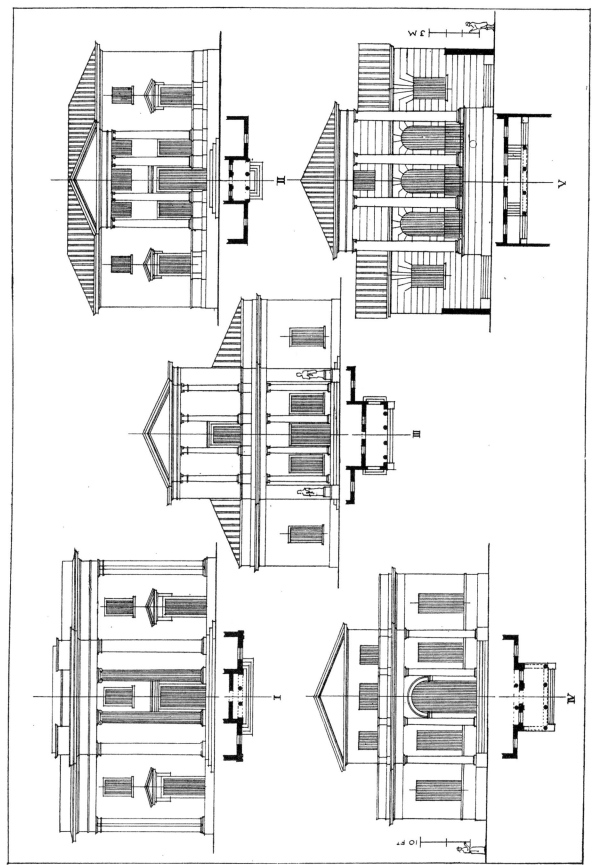

FACADES TWO STOREYS IN HEIGHT

GENERAL TYPES BASED ON ENGLISH AND ITALIAN PRACTICE.

I. BASED ON SEAFORTH HALL, LANCASHIRE, DESIGNED BY JAMES VALE.
II. EXAMPLE : CONSTABLE BURTON, YORKSHIRE, DESIGNED BY CARR OF YORK.

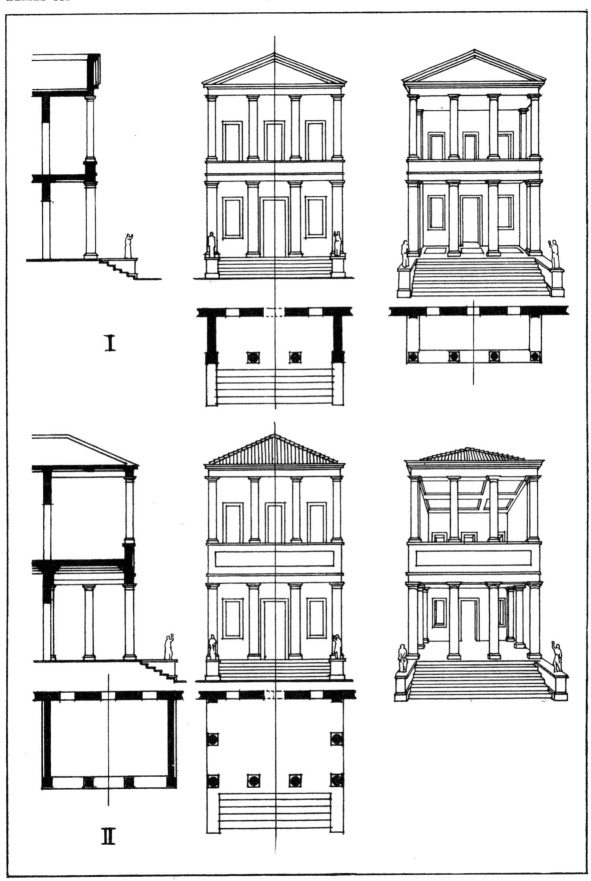

I

II

FACADES TWO STOREYS IN HEIGHT WITH OPEN LOGGIAS

GENERAL TYPES BASED ON ITALIAN PRACTICE.

FACADES WITH SCREENS AND VAULTED LOGGIAS

I-IV. GENERAL TYPES BASED ON ITALIAN PRACTICE.

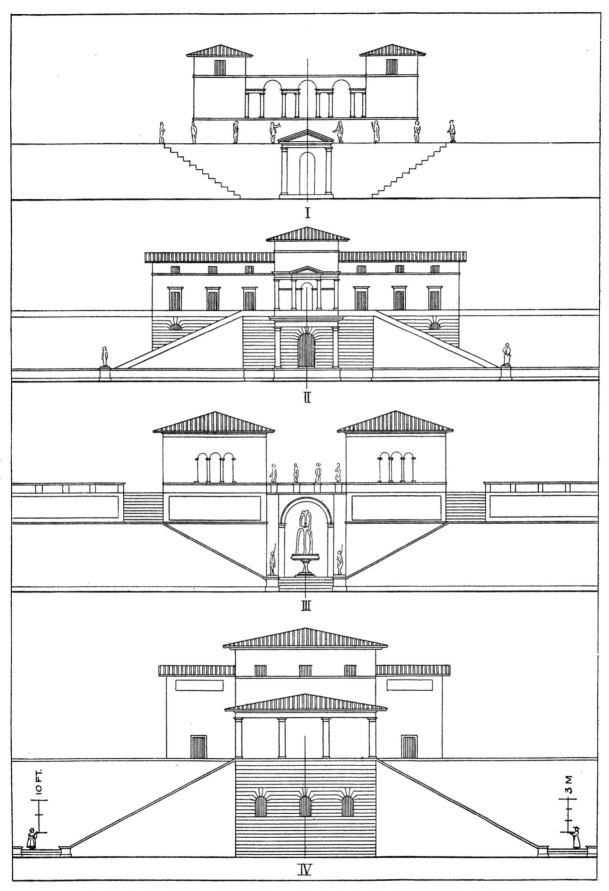

ITALIAN FACADES WITH LOGGIAS AND EXTERNAL STEPS

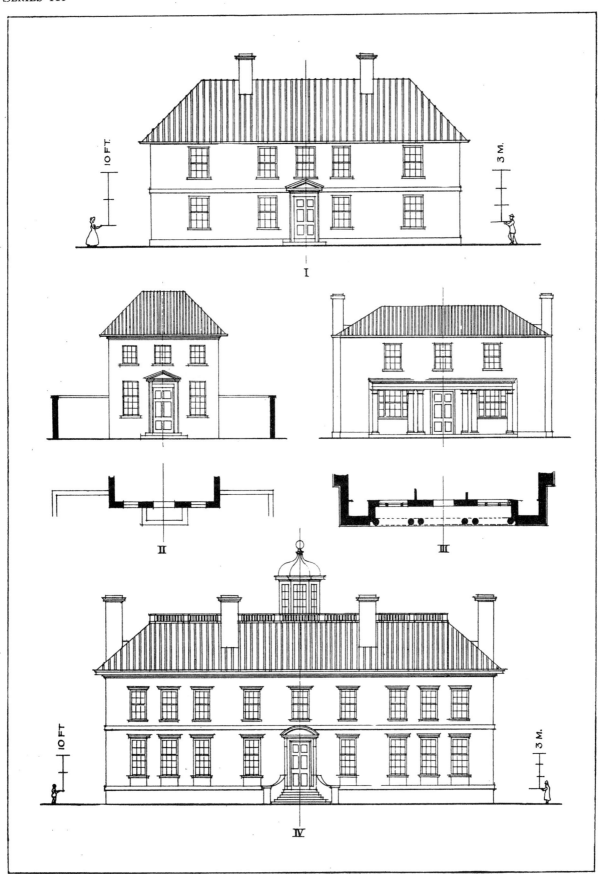

I

II

III

IV

FACADES TWO STOREYS IN HEIGHT
GENERAL TYPES BASED ON ENGLISH SEVENTEENTH AND EARLY EIGHTEENTH CENTURY PRACTICE.
IV. COLESHILL, BERKSHIRE, DESIGNED BY INIGO JONES.

185

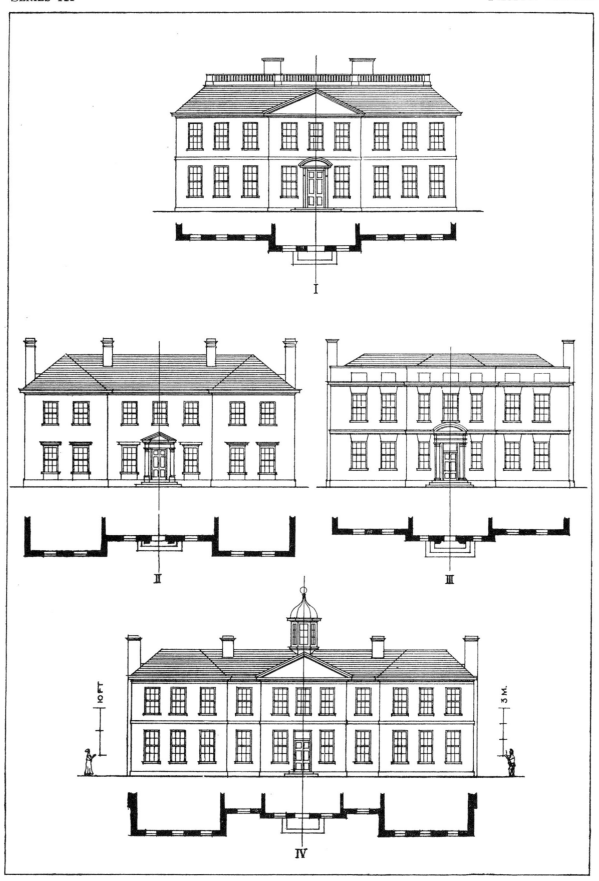

FACADES TWO STOREYS IN HEIGHT

GENERAL TYPES BASED ON ENGLISH SEVENTEENTH AND EARLY EIGHTEENTH CENTURY PRACTICE.

PLATE LXXXII

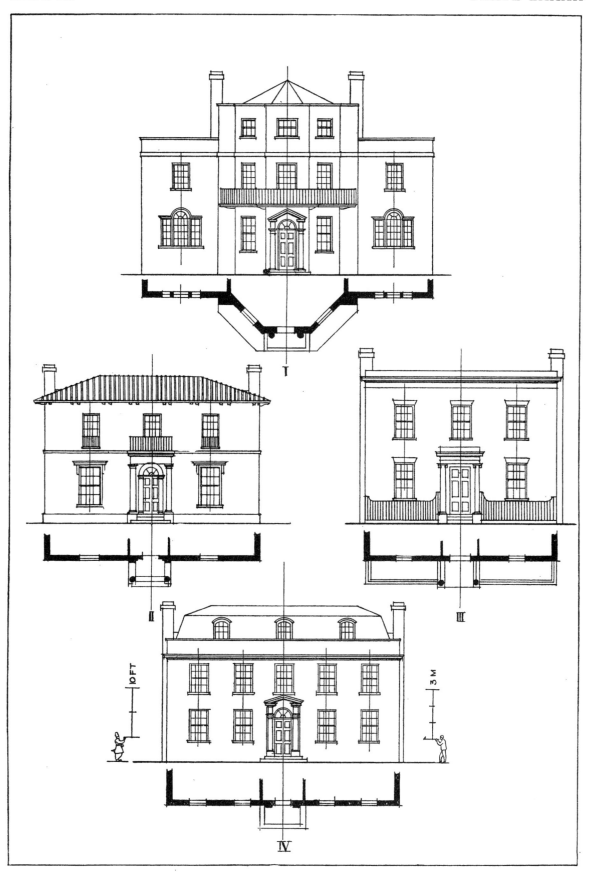

FACADES TWO PRINCIPAL STOREYS IN HEIGHT

GENERAL TYPES BASED ON ENGLISH LATE EIGHTEENTH CENTURY PRACTICE.

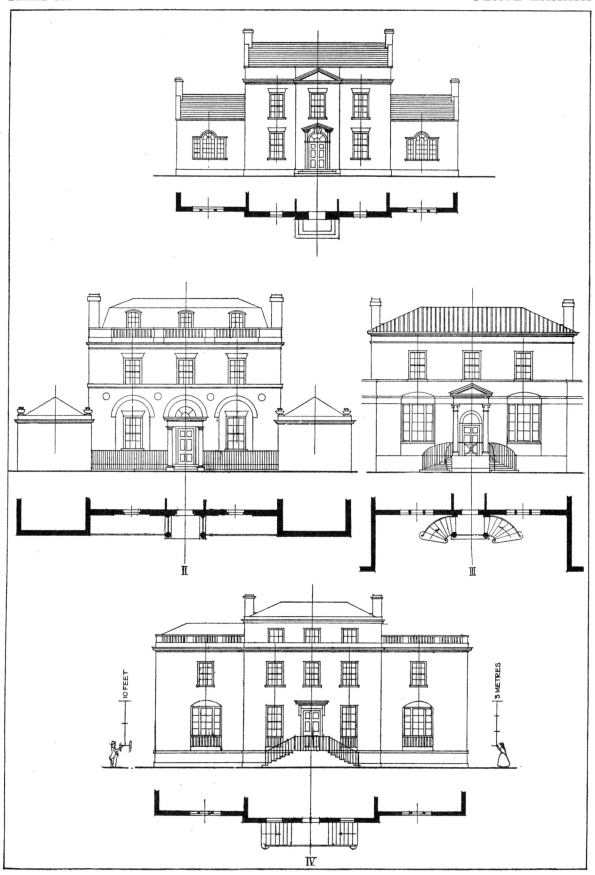

FACADES TWO PRINCIPAL STOREYS IN HEIGHT

GENERAL TYPES BASED ON ENGLISH LATE EIGHTEENTH CENTURY PRACTICE.

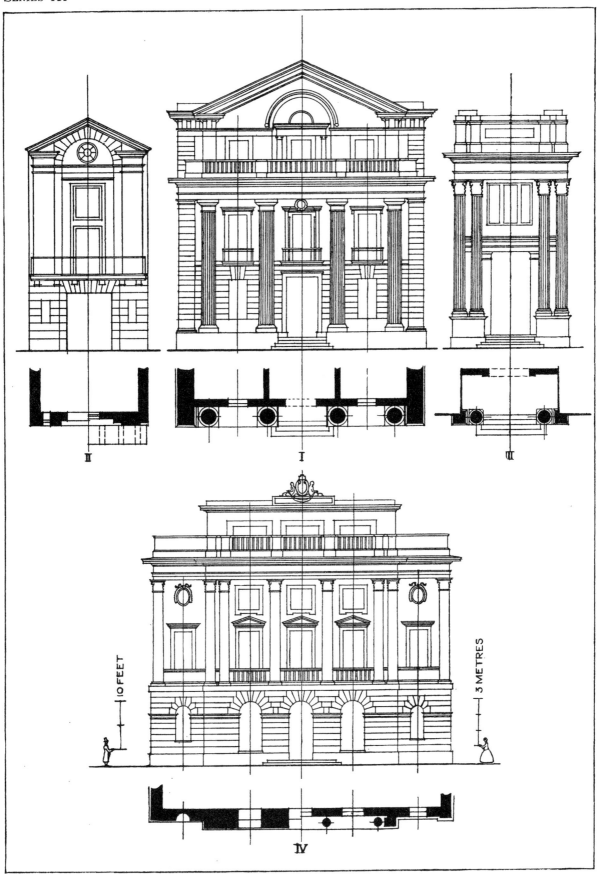

FACADES TWO PRINCIPAL STOREYS IN HEIGHT

I.   EXAMPLE : BANK OF ENGLAND, LIVERPOOL, DESIGNED BY C. R. COCKERELL, R.A.
II. EXAMPLE : AT VERSAILLES.
III. EXAMPLE : EXETER CHANGE, STRAND, LONDON (NO LONGER EXISTING).
IV. SOMERSLT HOUSE, LONDON (WELLINGTON STREET FRONT), DESIGNED BY SIR JAMES PENNETHORNE.

PLATE LXXXV

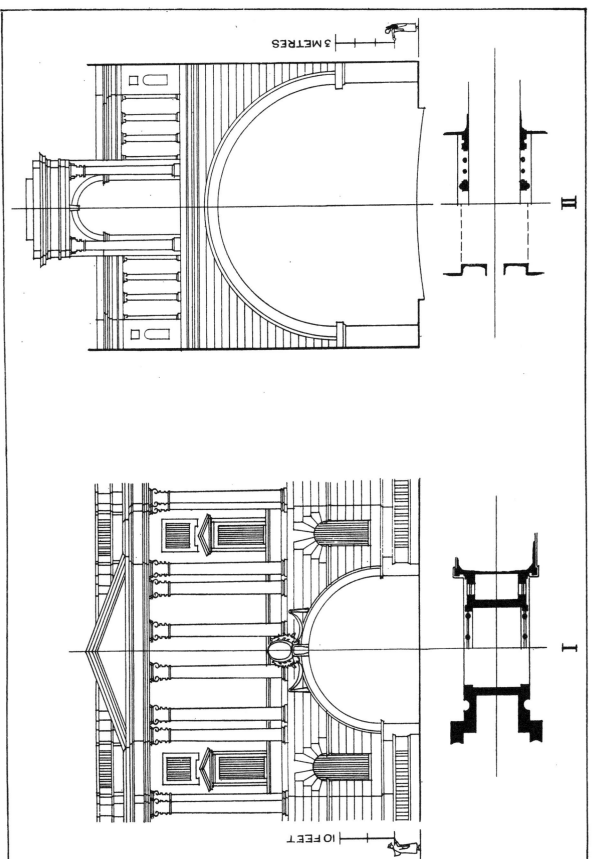

3 METRES

II

10 FEET

I

BRIDGE MOTIVES IN FACADE DESIGN

I. EXAMPLE : RIVER FRONT OF SOMERSET HOUSE, LONDON, DESIGNED BY SIR WILLIAM CHAMBERS.
II. EXAMPLE : THE REGENT'S BRIDGE, EDINBURGH, DESIGNED BY ARCHIBALD ELLIOT.

XII

PORTICOES AS FRONTISPIECES AND AS APPROACHES.

PLATES LXXXVI TO LXXXIX.

THE portico is characteristic of classic architecture in all countries and at all periods. Its purpose is three-fold : it is used (1) to provide shelter ; (2) to emphasise the main entrance to a building ; and (3) as a means of imparting dignity and character, at the same time producing effects of light and shade.

A portico may form an integral part of a building and express its mass as a whole ; or, it may be reduced to the status of a sub-motive of major interest ; or, the scale being relatively still further reduced, several porticoes may be introduced to serve as minor features with the object of enhancing the mass of a building. The proportions governing temple fronts have been generally followed for porticoes, but considerable licence in the disposition of columns, entablatures and pediments is characteristic of many of Renaissance origin.

Porticoes on a large scale express the unity of a building (Fig. 13). Classic temples, such as the Parthenon and other Greek peripteral buildings, and Roman examples, like the Maison Carrée at Nîmes, have been widely adapted to the requirements of later periods.

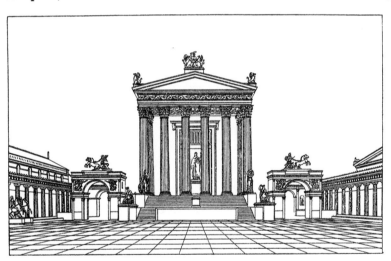

FIG. 13. PORTICO AS FRONTISPIECE TO A ROMAN TEMPLE.

The portico may be used singly, as the main feature of the façade of a building, permitting wide variety in the arrangement of the wall behind the projecting columns ; or, it may be used in two storeys, such as the double loggia ; while in the form of the porte-cochère it first came into use in France and England at the close of the eighteenth century. Other uses can be cited, such as at the entrances to mansions in town and country, and finally, as the minor features characteristic of the " Portico Period " a century ago, when a London house was considered to be incomplete without this type of entrance.

For buildings of large size, the portico with or without a crowning pediment should be further considered, first, as an attached feature with its arrangement of steps forming the chief interest and expression of a façade as in the front of the Church of St. Martin-in-the-Fields by James Gibbs; the National Gallery and University College, both by William Wilkins (see Plate XC for the plans of these); the Mansion House and the Royal Exchange, all in London, and St. George's Hall, Liverpool. Secondly, as a detached structure, used partly as a propylæum or gateway without an arch but with supporting pylons on either side, and partly as a screen. One of the best designs of this type with supporting colonnades is that of the Portico of Octavia, Rome, which dates from the Augustan age. Other outstanding instances of it are the Brandenburger Thor at Berlin by Langhans; the gateway and lodges at Euston Station, London

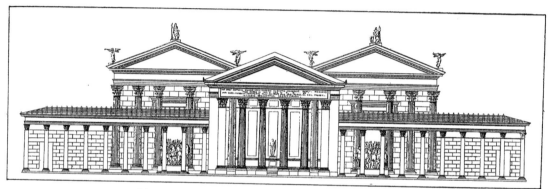

FIG. 14. RESTORATION OF THE PORTICO OF OCTAVIA, ROME, BY CANINA.

(Plate LXXXIX), by Thomas Hardwick; the entrance to Chester Castle by Thomas Harrison (Plate LXXXIX), and the gateway on Holyhead Harbour by the same architect.

Attention should also be directed to the attachment of porticoes to buildings, as well as to the arrangement and recessing of the wall surfaces that form their background. In this connection the porticoes of the Pantheon, Rome, the Panthéon, Paris (Plate LXXXVIII), and St. Paul's Cathedral, London (Plate LXXXVIII), should be studied, in all of which the vaulted ceiling is introduced. Another fine example is the façade of the Fitzwilliam Museum, Cambridge, by George Basevi, where the ceiling is flat coffered. This particular design is extremely interesting, and a study of its arrangement will show how a portico with pediment and flanking colonnades has been inset between supporting masses in the form of lofty pylons.

Another form of portico curved on plan was derived from the circular temple. It first made its appearance in Italy and France, and Sir Christopher Wren added semi-circular porticoes on a large scale to the transepts of St. Paul's Cathedral: later, James Gibbs used the same feature at the base of the tower of the Church of St. Mary-le-Strand, London. At the close of the eighteenth century, many English architects had recourse to French methods of planning, with the result that semi-circular porticoes were frequently introduced as minor features for country mansions.

In discussing porticoes, it has not been possible to define rigid principles for their application, neither is it convenient to separate them from the general series of elementary forms; many of the examples of façades illustrated in that series (Plates LXIX to LXXVI) exhibit a portico in some form or another.

Plate LXXXVI.—These general types summarise the usually accepted theories regarding the arrangement of columns to form porticoes which are frontispieces.

Plate LXXXVII.—This Plate shows two interesting three-part compositions with a central portico dominant in each.

Plate LXXXVIII.—Porticoes, when introduced as frontispieces, are sometimes designed with vaulted ceilings, following Roman precedent : this form of treatment allows of considerable variety in plan and section.

Plate LXXXIX.—When a portico is used as an entrance to a courtyard or forecourt it serves both as a frontispiece and as a monumental gateway. The examples in this Plate are characteristic adaptions of this essentially classic feature.

REFERENCE BOOKS.

Bühlmann, J. *Architektur des Klassichen Altertums und der Renaissance.* 1904.
Hittorff, C. *Les Antiquités Inedites de l'Attique.* 1832.
Lowell, Guy. *Small Italian Villas and Farmhouses.*
Stuart, J., and Revett, N. *The Antiquities of Athens.* 1762-1832.
Richardson, A. E. *Monumental Architecture in Great Britain.* 1914.

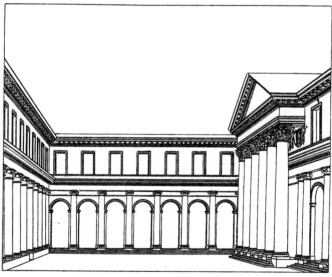

FIG. 15. PORTICO IN THE COURTYARD OF THE OLD SCHOOL OF MEDECINE, PARIS.

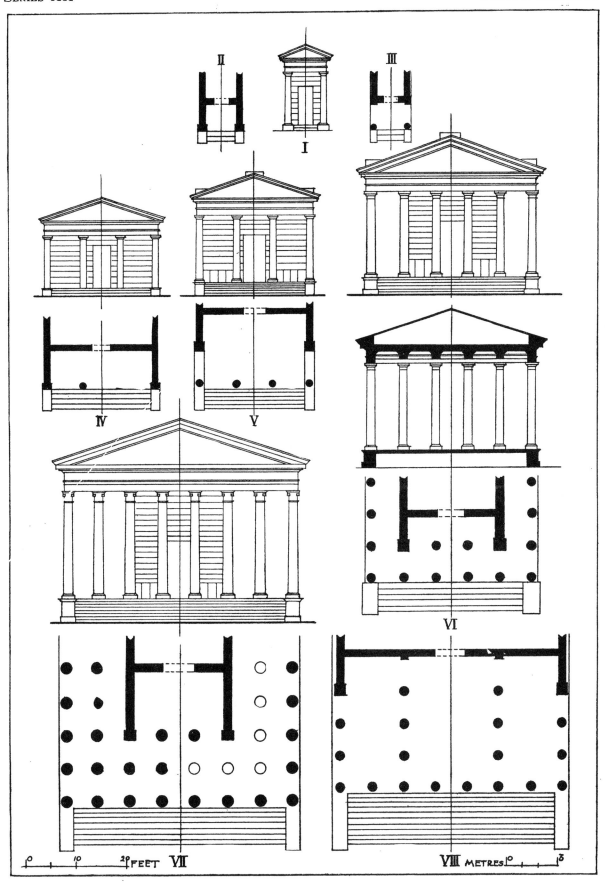

PORTICOES AS FRONTISPIECES

I-VIII.   GENERAL TYPES BASED ON AUTHENTIC EXAMPLES.

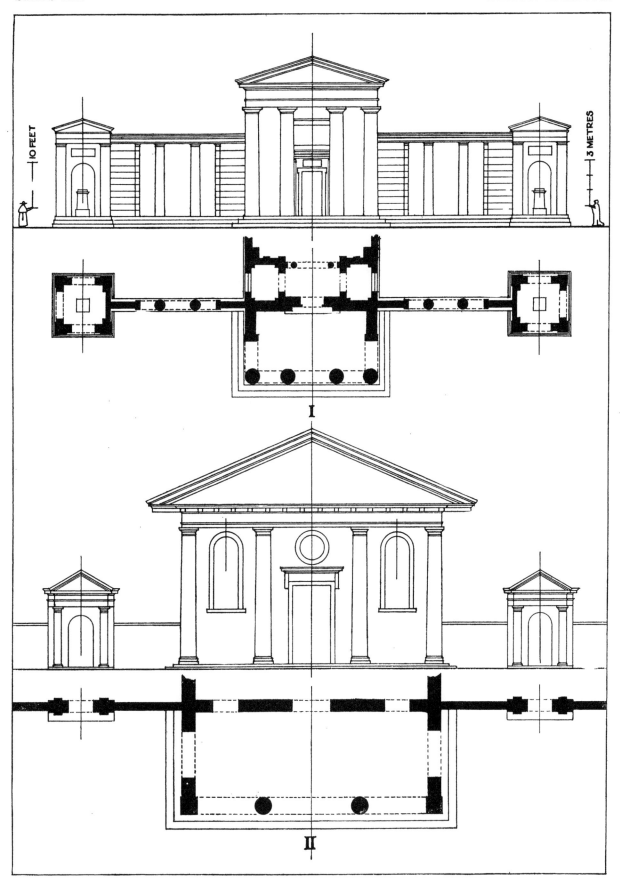

PORTICOES AS FRONTISPIECES

I.   EXAMPLE : CHURCH OF AYOT ST. LAWRENCE, HERTFORDSHIRE, DESIGNED BY NICHOLAS, REVETT.
II.   BASED ON CHURCH OF ST. PAUL, COVENT GARDEN, LONDON, DESIGNED BY INIGO JONES.

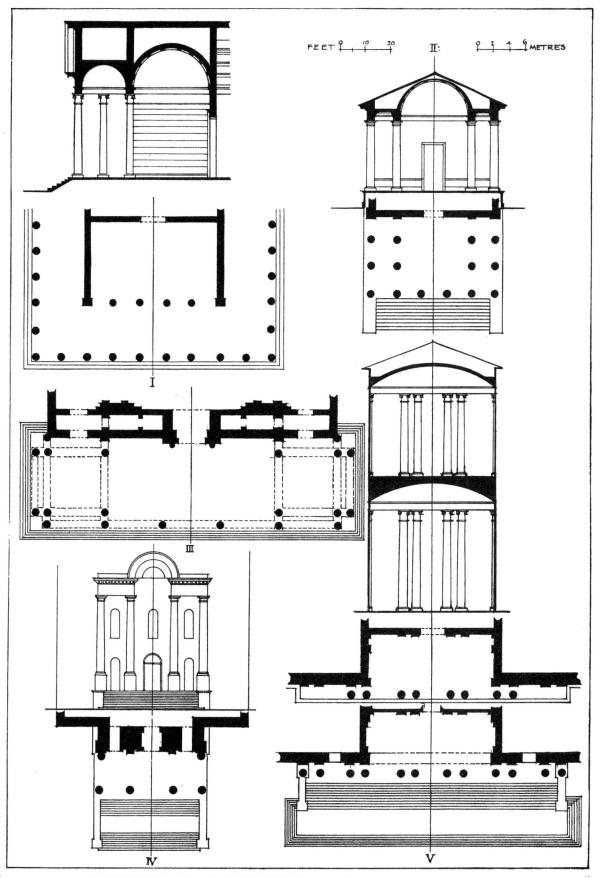

FEET 0   10   20   II: 0 2 4 6 METRES

PORTICOES AS FRONTISPIECES WITH VAULTED CEILINGS

I-II.   GENERAL TYPES BASED ON ROMAN PRACTICE.

III.   EXAMPLE : THE PANTHEON, PARIS, DESIGNED BY J. G. SOUFFLOT.

IV.   EXAMPLE : CHRISTCHURCH, SPITALFIELDS, LONDON, DESIGNED BY NICHOLAS HAWKSMOOR.

V.   EXAMPLE : WEST FRONT OF ST. PAUL'S CATHEDRAL, DESIGNED BY SIR CHRISTOPHER WREN.

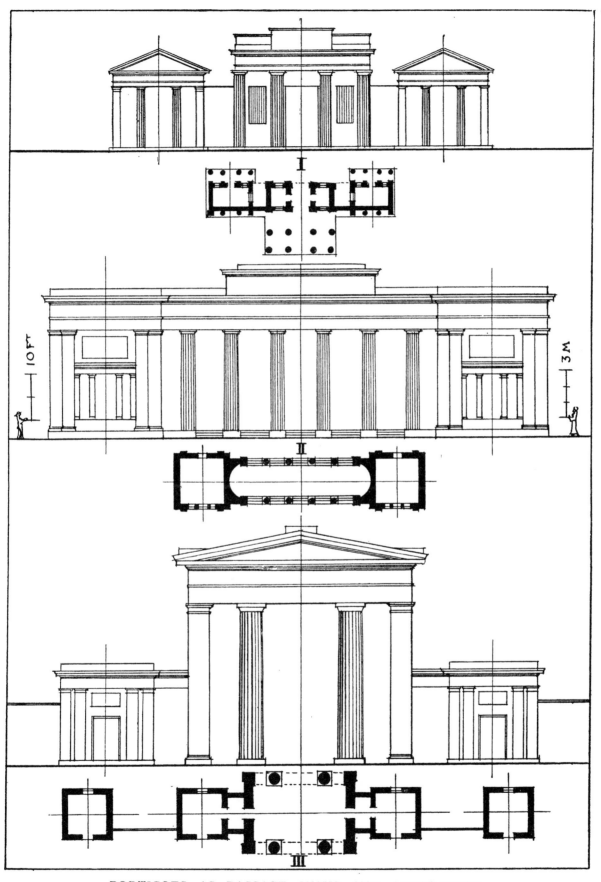

PORTICOES AS PASSAGE WAYS AND APPROACHES

I.   EXAMPLE: THE CASTLE, CHESTER, DESIGNED BY THOMAS HARRISON.
II. BASED ON THE CORN EXCHANGE, LONDON, DESIGNED BY GEORGE SMITH.
III. EXAMPLE: APPROACH TO EUSTON STATION, LONDON, DESIGNED BY THOMAS HARDWICK.

XIII

EXTERNAL STEPS AND STAIRCASES.

PLATES XC AND XCI.

MANY theories have been advanced in the past about the external staircase as a feature in the design of buildings. In practice, climatic conditions inevitably decide the type of design most suitable.

There is everything to be gained both for effect and for convenience by introducing a main stepped approach to the principal floor of a building directly from the street level or from a courtyard. This is largely a question of design in a specific building programme and admits of great variety of treatment. Classic architecture in England is prolific in examples of external approaches, which came into use in a minor way at the close of the seventeenth century (Fig. 16), but it was not till after about the year 1730 that they were freely introduced for buildings of large scale. Lord Burlington in his villa at Chiswick, near London, employed an elaborate stepped approach ; George Dance, the Elder, contrived a double staircase at the extremities of the portico to the Mansion House, London (which has since been altered), and throughout the latter half of the eighteenth century many country mansions were given this distinctive feature. In the early part of the nineteenth century the ingenuity of William Wilkins, R.A., produced two unique designs for the National Gallery and University College, London, the one contained within the line of the projecting portico, and the other carried boldly beyond it : both are illustrated on the first Plate of this Series.

In the middle of the nineteenth century a novelty was introduced in the design of the Museum at Berlin where Schinkel devised an external staircase immediately within the open colonnade, and many years later this motive was followed by Poleart at the Palais de Justice, Brussels.

Plate XC.—No. I shows a plain flight of steps with " returned " ends. No. II is the orthodox treatment of a flight of steps between wing walls, arranged in front of a hexastyle portico. No. III is an ingenious triple flight arranged directly in front of a recessed colonnade, the object being to economise space. No. IV shows a form of triple approach in which the steps enter the ends of the portico. No. V is a more extravagant disposition of triple flights. No. VI, which is taken from the principal quadrangle of University College, London, is chiefly notable for the treatment of the walls to the steps in such a way that they serve the dual purpose of breaking the flights to economise space and at the same time become groupings subordinate to the podium.   No. VII is drawn from the National Gallery, London, and follows the same principle as No. VI : both these examples show a masterly departure from precedent.

Plate XCI.—Figs. I to III show the treatment for steps of curvilinear and semi-circular plan, ranging from the shaped " curtail " steps peculiar to all phases of eighteenth century architecture, and the semi-circular flight leading directly to an entrance without columns, to the semi-circular steps and portico on a grand scale, designed by Sir Christopher Wren.   In No. IV, quadrant flights form a double approach to a central landing, the whole being kept free from the building.   No. V is a double semi-circular motive combined with a central portico landing : a very effective arrangement where space is available. No. VI shows a segmental disposition of steps and colonnade together with a segmental feature forming part of the main building.   No. VII is an example of double semi-circular flights of steps introduced at the ends of a tetrastyle portico, with which it combines gracefully.

FIG. 16.   EXTERNAL STEPS AT BROADWAY,
WORCESTERSHIRE.

PLATE XC

SERIES XIII

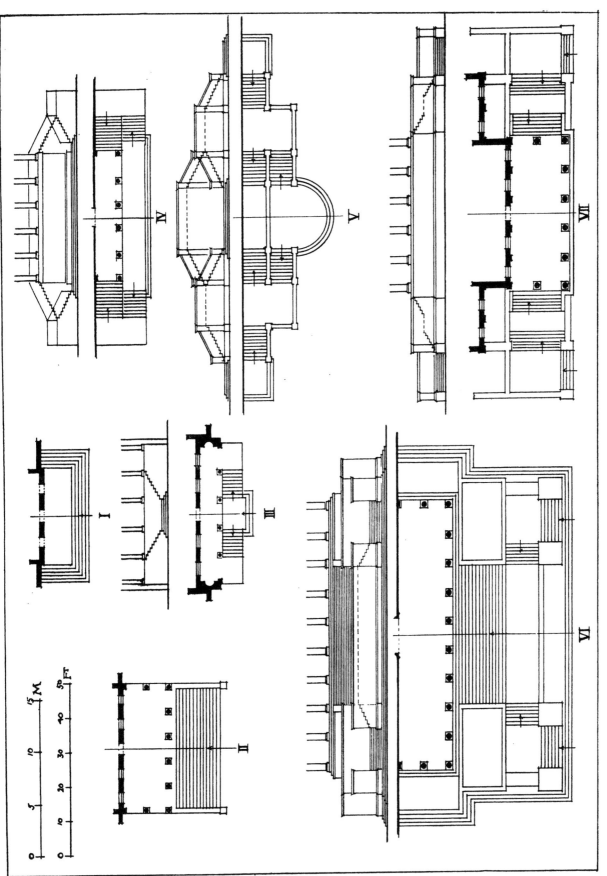

EXTERNAL STAIRCASES AND STEPS IN STRAIGHT AND "RETURNED" FLIGHTS

I-V.   GENERAL TYPES BASED ON ENGLISH AND FRENCH EIGHTEENTH CENTURY PRACTICE.
VI.   EXAMPLE : APPROACH TO PORTICO, UNIVERSITY COLLEGE, LONDON, DESIGNED BY WILLIAM WILKINS, R.A.
VII.   EXAMPLE : APPROACH TO THE NATIONAL GALLERY, LONDON, DESIGNED BY WILLIAM WILKINS, R.A.

PLATE XCI

EXTERNAL STAIRCASES AND STEPS OF CURVILINEAR PLAN

I-VI. GENERAL TYPES BASED ON ENGLISH EIGHTEENTH CENTURY PRACTICE.

XIV

TRIUMPHAL ARCHES, GATEWAYS AND PORCHES.

PLATES XCII TO XCIV.

THE triumphal arch, as evolved by the Romans, must be considered primarily as a commemorative monument. There are many variants of the type, both trabeated and arcuated, which can be sub-divided into groups, such as those consisting of a single archway, of which the Arch of Titus, Rome, is a notable example : the triple archway, consisting of a central opening with subordinate arches, of which the Arch of Constantine, Rome, is one of the best examples ; and minor types of double archways unified by an attic storey. There are also certain trabeated triumphal arches, such as the Arch of the Goldsmiths, Rome. Amongst notable modern examples are the Arc de Triomphe, Paris, by Chalgrin, the Triumphal Arch at Petrograd, designed by Querenghi (Plate XCII), and that at Madison Square, New York, by McKim.

During the sixteenth century in Italy, the principle of the triumphal arch was adapted to form a central motive of certain types of façade. Throughout the ensuing phases of the Renaissance in France, including the period of the Empire, this feature constantly recurs in buildings of the first importance, modified in detail, but following the accepted disposition. From 1830 till 1880 the French Grand Prix designs reveal an insistence on the theory of an arched motive for central masses as a variation of the more usual portico front.

In England, the triumphal arch was seldom applied as a central feature in a range of buildings. It was adopted to some extent by Sir William Chambers and the school of the brothers Adam for screens and ornamental gateways ; it was used in its entirety by Sir John Soane to form part of the Lothbury Court of the Bank of England, and is found again in his design for the completion of the Treasury, Whitehall.

After 1815, the triumphal arch appeared in London as an isolated monument. John Nash designed the Marble Arch and erected it as the chief feature in the courtyard of Buckingham Palace, whence it was afterwards removed to its present site. In the entrance at Hyde Park Corner Decimus Burton employed the triumphal arch in triple form connected by screens, but the design is not entirely satisfactory owing to lack of rhythm. His arch on Constitution Hill is the finest example in London.

Reference should be made to the buildings of the eighteenth century in France and also to the Grand Prix designs for further insight into the application of the triumphal arch motive.

There is yet another purpose to which isolated arched features, which are not purely utilitarian, can be applied : this concerns temporary street decorations for processions and state pageants.   Arches of this description have been erected in England from the time of Inigo Jones to the present day, and instances of their effective use can be seen in French, American and other works which touch on this subject.   A fine example is reproduced in Fig. 17.

Plate XCII.—This shows two examples in which the arch is treated in a highly decorative way.   The upper one, attributed to Clérisseau, shows how a dominant archway may be connected with quadrant screens.   The other example, in which the arch is subordinate, relies for its effect on the grouping of the columns on the various faces.   In this design the columnar treatment is dominant.

FIG. 17.   A TEMPORARY TRIUMPHAL ARCH SET UP IN PARIS, DESIGNED BY PERCIER AND FONTAINE.

GATEWAYS.

Monumental gateways generally form central features opening into court-yards. In such cases they should be schemed to form subsidiary focal points, besides complementing the architecture of the buildings adjacent to them.

Entrances of this kind follow three main types based on the following principles :—I, Trabeation ; II, Arcuation, and III, the " Palladian " motive. There are many possible variations of these : for example, the entrance to the Cortile of an Italian Palace, to the French Cour d'Honneur, and numerous English treatments such as those of the " Porta Honoris " at Caius College, Cambridge ; the Water-gate of old York House, London, by Inigo Jones ; the Middle Temple Gateway and old Temple Bar, by Sir Christopher Wren ; the gateway at Queen's College, Oxford, by Nicholas Hawksmoor, and the fine gateways at the extremities of the courtyard of Somerset House, by Sir William Chambers.

Plate XCIII.—These examples, drawn from widely differing sources, show trabeated and arcuated forms and combinations of both.

PORCHES.

The treatment of porches must be considered from two points of view, first as forming the approach to a building and affording protection from the weather, and secondly in relation to the design of façades in which a porch usually forms the focal point. In towns the projection of porches is determined by the site, width of pavement and other considerations, and many ingenious arrangements have been employed to secure the maximum projection without unduly encroach-ing upon the public way. Porches are sometimes quite plain, but more usually they have columns—engaged or standing free—and pilasters carrying an entablature and surmounted by a pediment or balustrade. The width and depth of a porch are designed to suit the particular building of which it forms part : short flights of steps add to the distinction of an entrance, serving as introductory features and connecting the focal point to the general lines of the building. Nearly every city in Europe and America shows a variety of treatments peculiar to local practice, but reminiscent in their general lines of the classic models by which their forms were suggested.

There are examples of circular porches which produce grandeur of effect, such as those to the transepts of St. Paul's Cathedral. The small example in Lincoln's Inn Fields (Plate XCIV, No. VIII), designed by Sir John Soane, is unique, inasmuch as it preserves the unity of the façade and at the same time masks a dual entrance. Many variations of form based on the square and the circle can be designed to suit special circumstances.

The porches and entrance doorways of London offer a wide field for investigating the diversity of types familiar to the eighteenth and early nineteenth centuries; and no better way could be suggested for the study of this particular element of design than to sketch one example of each type encountered in the streets of the Metropolis. Paris is also rich in examples of this period, and the eighteenth century in America produced entrances of the portico type which contain novel features drawn from French and English sources. Reference to the treatise by Krafft on the porches and porte-cochères of Paris will show how the porch was treated by celebrated French architects.

Plate XCIV.—A simple porch with pediment is shown in No. I, in which the columns are disengaged and stand either close in front of pilasters, as shown in plan and section, or at a distance from them not exceeding three-quarters of their distance apart, as shown in plan and section No. II, the elevation being unchanged. The elevation and section of a simple porch following in principle the type of No. I, but without a pediment, is given in No. III, the plans No. II applying equally to it. Nos. IV and V show the plan and elevation of a porch having four columns in front, and No. VI the plan of one with four columns in front and one on each return, giving a richer effect when viewed in perspective. Plan No. VII shows a disposition of three bays formed of coupled columns standing in front of pilasters engaged with the main wall : this is especially suited to lengthy façades, and a notable example of its application occurs in the work of John Nash at No. 29 Dover Street, W. The plan of a semi-circular porch designed to mask a double entrance and at the same time to preserve its entity as a single feature is given in No. VIII. The elevation of a projecting porch with columns engaged at the angles is given in No. IX. It is a type suited to conditions where an effect of strength is needed, and may be used when an inner vestibule is required.

Students should avoid multiplying unnecessary features in the design of porches, and should eliminate as far as possible heavy rustications, key-stones, festoons, and other decorations, which tend to detract from the simplicity of expression which is desirable. The design of entrances on a large scale, such as the river entrance to Somerset House (Plate LXXXV), detached gateways (Plate XCIII), and features in open screens (Plate XCVII) demands separate study.

REFERENCE BOOKS.

Krafft, J. *Porte Cochères de Paris.* 1838.
Gourlier. *Choix d'Edifices Publics.* 1825-36.

TRIUMPHAL ARCHES AND GATEWAYS

I. COMPOSITION ATTRIBUTED TO CLERISSEAU, FROM AN ORIGINAL DRAWING IN THE LIBRARY OF THE ROYAL INSTITUTE
OF BRITISH ARCHITECTS.

II. TRIUMPHAL ARCH AT PETROGRAD, DESIGNED BY GIACOMO QUARENGHI.

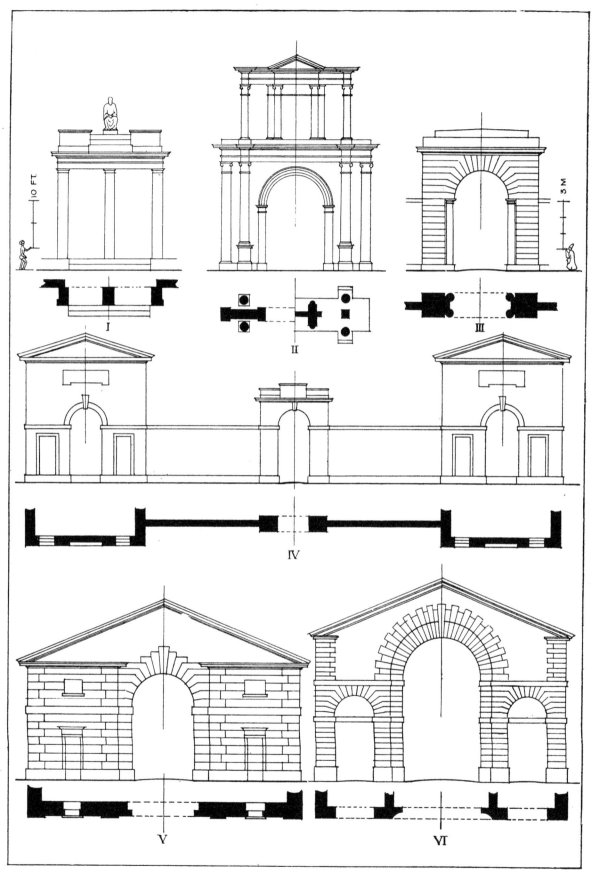

GATEWAYS

I-II.   BASED ON GREEK EXAMPLES.
III-IV.   GENERAL TYPES BASED ON ENGLISH EIGHTEENTH CENTURY PRACTICE.
V-VI.   GENERAL TYPES BASED ON FRENCH SEVENTEENTH AND EIGHTEENTH CENTURY PRACTICE.

219

PORCHES

I-X.   GENERAL TYPES BASED ON ENGLISH EIGHTEENTH CENTURY PRACTICE.

XV

SCREENS AND COLONNADES.

PLATES XCV TO XCVIII.

THE functional value of the screen determines its design : it is either a link between two masses, with or without a strong central feature ; or it can be treated as a skeleton façade of dominant interest with a central motive based upon the triumphal arch, or with dual entrances near the extremities. Screens are introduced into the composition of buildings for completing circulation in plans and for providing covered thoroughfares without interfering with axial lines or means of approach. They are capable of being treated in one or more storeys, and they are used either to complete the fourth side of a quadrangle or Court of Honour, thus enabling architectural lines to be continued and the extent of a whole scheme to be comprehended : or, in special cases, to mask central façades which retreat between wings, as at the Admiralty, Whitehall (Plate XCVI, No. III), where Robert Adam designed the screen to reduce the apparent height of Ripley's ungainly portico. Another general use for a single storey screen is to ensure additional privacy to a courtyard, as in the other examples on the same Plate from the Palace of Compiègne and from Carlton House, W.

In the eighteenth century, no building of importance or entrance to a nobleman's park was considered to be complete without some form of architectural screen with which lodges and gates were combined. Such screens generally consist of a single row of columns strengthened either at the centre or at the extremities by projecting masses : the screen at Syon House, Isleworth (Plate XCVII), is an outstanding example of the matured development of this application. Further, screens may be open below with a closed storey above, as at the old School of Medicine, Paris (Plate XCVIII).

During the Renaissance period in Italy the recognised practice of architects was to provide arcaded or colonnaded screens sympathetic with the façades of the buildings of which they form part, and examples of façades incorporating such features are given on Plate LXXVIII.

Although, broadly speaking, the composition of the screen in its general massing is limited to certain definite arrangements, considerable variety is available to the designer, as will be seen from reference to the Plates in this series and to some of the minor examples extant in London and other cities.

Internal screens were effectively introduced in halls and rooms of large size throughout the Renaissance period in all countries. Their functions are varied and their scenic value undisputed. In England, during the eighteenth century especially, many fine designs for internal screens were evolved, and an interesting modification is seen in the columns carrying arches or entablatures to screen the ends of large rooms in public buildings, or the curved ends of reception rooms in dwelling-houses. Reference to the example from the Bank of England on Plate XXXII, and from town houses designed by the Brothers Adam and others on Plate XXXIII, will show this application of the screen motive. Many designs by French architects may also be referred to, while the pictorial compositions drawn by such Italian masters as Bibiena, Pannini and Piranesi (Plate LIV), show how the use of screens for interior effect was generally accepted : a good example by an unknown artist is reproduced on Plate XCV.

Plate XCVI.—The beautiful colonnaded screen at the Palace of Compiègne, with pedimented opening at the centre and pylons at the extremities, is shown in No. I. The screen formerly fronting Carlton House, London, is given in elevation in No. II and in perspective on Plate XCV. In this fine example, the columns are coupled, and additional importance is given to the dual gateways by the introduction of intermediate and terminating pylons. No. III shows the Admiralty Screen, Whitehall, which consists of a grouping of three masses : the colonnade is arranged in front of a blind wall and binds, through the agency of its entablature, the three main motives of the design.

Plate XCVII.—No. I shows a screen of columns forming an open colonnade, unified at the centre by means of an arched opening of attic form. The screen shown in No. II is formed of single columns with an arched opening at the centre, and is terminated at the extremities by square masses having sympathetic cornices. No. III shows a single screen with two arched openings flanked by coupled columns, with a small doorway for pedestrians in each of the short wings.

Plate XCVIII.—An open screen of columns giving a central way for wheeled traffic, and two openings for pedestrians, is given in No. I : it is an example of extreme simplicity and grace. Fig. II represents the famous screen placed in advance of a number of doorways and forming a loggia at Hampton Court Palace, designed by Sir Christopher Wren : the coupled columns are carefully adjusted between wing walls to give rhythm to seven bays. The screen used in a complex manner is shown in No. III : in this design will be found a fine solution of the problem of connecting two groups of buildings across the face of an open courtyard, where it is necessary to leave the ground floor comparatively open and to provide circulation under cover at an upper level.

REFERENCE BOOKS.

Gourlier. *Choix d'Edifices Publics.* 1825-36.
Planat, P. *Le Style Louis XVI.*
Compositions by Piranesi, Bibiena and other Italian Masters.

COLUMNAR SCREENS

I.   EXTERNAL SCREEN.   CARLTON HOUSE, LONDON, DESIGNED BY HENRY HOLLAND.   (NO LONGER EXISTING.)
(See also Plate XCVI)

II.   INTERNAL SCREEN IN A COMPOSITION BY AN UNKNOWN ARTIST.   FROM AN ORIGINAL DRAWING IN THE LIBRARY OF THE
ROYAL INSTITUTE OF BRITISH ARCHITECTS.

PLATE XCVI

SERIES XV

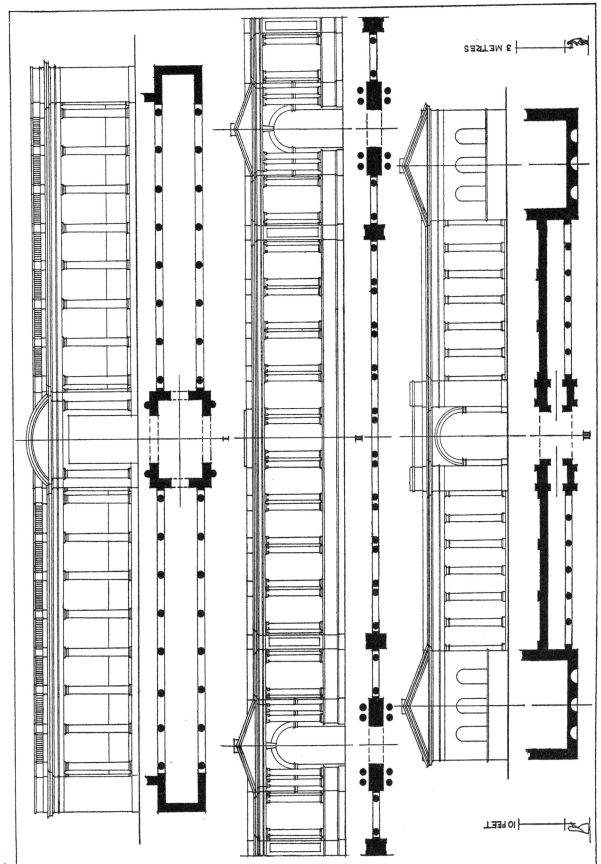

EXTERNAL COLONNADED SCREENS

I. EXAMPLE : PALACE OF COMPIÈGNE, DESIGNED BY J. A. GABRIEL.
II. EXAMPLE : CARLTON HOUSE, LONDON (NO LONGER EXISTING), DESIGNED BY HENRY HOLLAND.
III. THE ADMIRALTY, WHITEHALL, LONDON, DESIGNED BY THE BROTHERS ADAM.

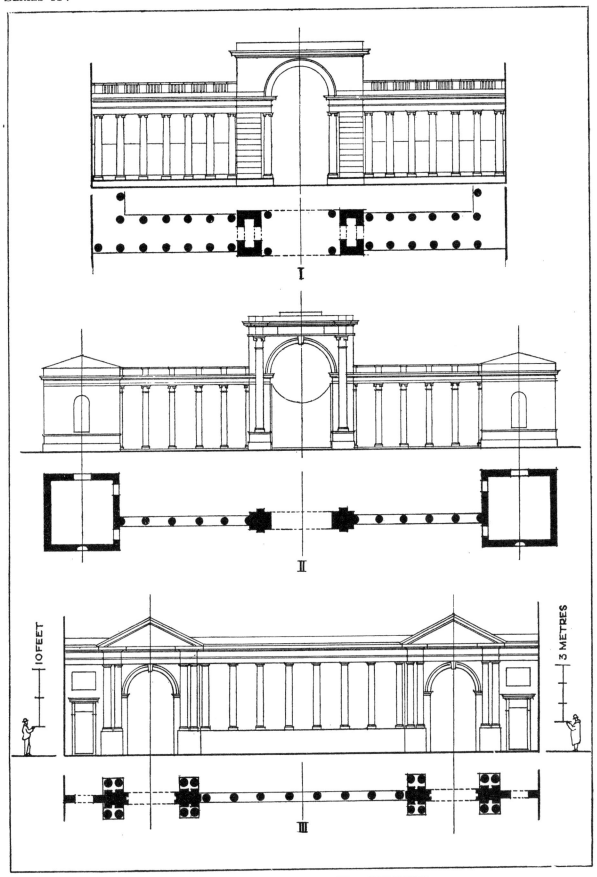

EXTERNAL COLONNADED SCREENS

I.   EXAMPLE : HOTEL DE SALM, PARIS, DESIGNED BY PIERRE ROUSSEAU.

II. EXAMPLE : SYON HOUSE, ISLEWORTH, MIDDLESEX, DESIGNED BY THE BROTHERS ADAM.

III. EXAMPLE : GROSVENOR HOUSE, LONDON, DESIGNED BY THOMAS CUNDY.

PLATE XCVIII

EXTERNAL COLONNADED SCREENS

I.   EXAMPLE : METROPOLITAN CLUB, NEW YORK, DESIGNED BY MCKIM.
II. EXAMPLE : HAMPTON COURT PALACE, DESIGNED BY SIR CHRISTOPHER WREN.
III. EXAMPLE : OLD ECOLE DE MÉDECINE, PARIS, DESIGNED BY J. GONDOUIN.

3 METRES

10 FEET

XVI

GROTTOES.

PLATES XCIX AND C.

THIS series includes features which belong essentially to the ornamental aspect of architectural design. The grotto is used as a feature of embellishment in parks and public places remote from the centre of the city, and also to ornament gardens and parks on private estates. Various treatments are peculiar to the Continent and the theory of the grotto has not been overlooked in England, but of recent years insufficient attention has been paid by architects to this subject with the result that treatments of rock-work have been allowed to usurp the distinctive character which properly belongs to such a structure. The grotto, whatever its treatment as an individual motive, should be considered as forming the culmination of a series of incidents connected with the display of ornamental water. Theoretically, in the innermost groves of a park, there should be a source either in the form of a spring or a cistern : the water would then be conducted to a stream which further on becomes a cascade with suitable falls, passing from a naturalistic setting to a long canal, whence it would descend over another cascade on conventional lines and finally to the grotto : a group of fountains beyond the grotto would mark the furthest extent to which the water is carried.

In the formation of the grotto, advantage is taken of the natural fall of the ground to build at a point which readily affords more than one level. The plan form usually favoured is based upon the hemicycle, with subsidiary recesses, while ranges of steps, columnar screens and symbolic statuary play an important part in the grouping. Where marked differences of level do not occur, the grotto should be treated on more conventional lines, as is the case in the gardens at Versailles, where a screen surrounds a basin with a central fountain.

The grotto on a small scale is best designed to form part of its natural surroundings, in which case highly conventional forms give place to simpler and more natural arrangements in accord with the character of the earth and rocks. Reference to the grottoes in innumerable gardens adjoining important villas in Italy (Fig. 18) should enable the student to master the characteristic treatments and to select suitable architectural detail and sculpture. In this series of illustrations eight examples are given, and although the subject cannot here be dealt with in greater detail, sufficient information is given for the designer to appreciate the relative importance of the subject.

Plate XCIX.—No I is an illustration of a grotto formed in the hill-side between two levels : it is of the hemicycle type with an interior screen of columns

masking niches planned on the radial lines, the double staircase meeting above
the entrance. No. II shows a more complex rendering, the chief feature being
a colonnade combined with dual stairways to the higher level. No. III shows
another of the hemicycle type with a screen of columns and stepped approach.
No. IV follows the same theory, but includes subordinate niches and a vaulted
loggia. No. V consists of an arcaded and saucer domed loggia of three bays
with five semi-circular recesses. No. VI shows a simple recess forming a feature
in an arcaded and domed loggia : this type could be introduced at recurring
intervals. No. VII combines elements of all the foregoing in a grand scheme of
grotto, canal, basin, fountain and steps.

Plate C.—This composition is introduced for the architectural treatment of
a grotto and fountain forming a centre of interest between two levels, such as
might be encountered in the lay-out of public grounds. The dual stairway is
arranged between walls clear of the semi-circular colonnade and reaches the
higher level above the central recess, thereby giving access to an avenue at the
higher level and enabling the upper part of the colonnade to form a terrace.

REFERENCE BOOKS.

Durand, J. N. L. *Précis des Leçons d'Architecture*. 1802-9.
Triggs, H. I. *The Art of Garden Design in Italy*. 1906.

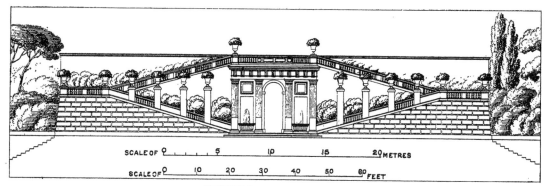

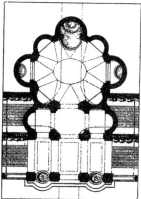

FIG. 18. GROTTO IN THE GARDEN OF THE PALAZZO PALLAVICINO, GENOA.

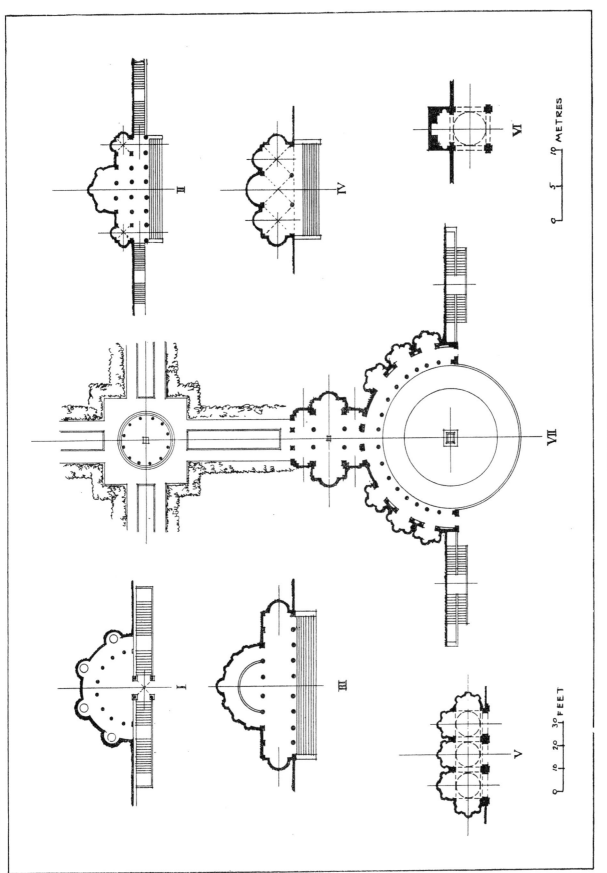

GROTTOES

GENERAL TYPES BASED ON ITALIAN PRACTICE.

I

II

III

IV

V

VI

VII

0 5 10 METRES

0 10 20 30 FEET

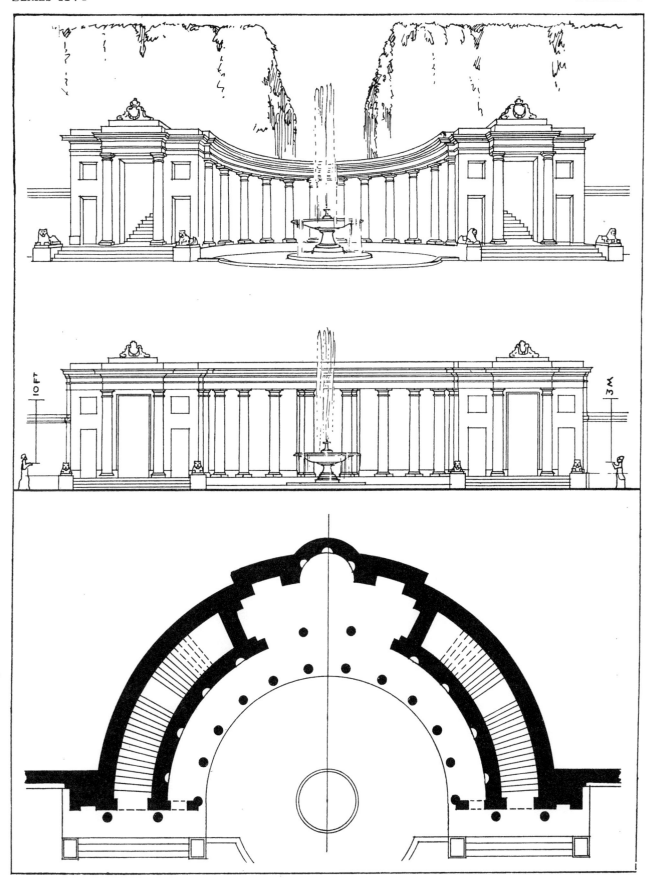

GROTTO

PLAN, ELEVATION AND SKETCH, BASED ON A DESIGN BY M. J. PEYRE.

INDEX TO ILLUSTRATIONS.

The larges numerals, thus XXVI, *refer to plate numbers. The small numerals, thus* iv,
*indicate the particular diagrams on the plate referred to. The illustrations referred to
thus, Fig. 8, will be found in the text.*